The Executive
Decisionmaking
Process

The Executive Decisionmaking Process

Identifying Problems and Assessing Outcomes

RALPH SANDERS

QUORUM BOOKS
Westport, Connecticut • London

Library of Congress Cataloging-in-Publication Data

Sanders, Ralph.
  The executive decisionmaking process : identifying problems and
assessing outcomes / Ralph Sanders.
    p. cm.
  Includes bibliographical references and index.
  ISBN 1–56720–293–4 (alk. paper)
  1. Decision making. 2. Problem solving. 3. Management—Decision
making. 4. Executives. I. Title. II. Title: Executive decision
making process.
  HD30.23.S2495   1999
  658.4'03—dc21   99–13715

British Library Cataloguing in Publication Data is available.

Library of Congress Catalog Card Number: 99–13715
ISBN: 1–56720–293–4

First published in 1999

Quorum Books, 88 Post Road West, Westport, CT 06881
An imprint of Greenwood Publishing Group, Inc.
www.quorumbooks.com

Printed in the United States of America

The paper used in this book complies with the
Permanent Paper Standard issued by the National
Information Standards Organization (Z39.48–1984).

10 9 8 7 6 5 4 3 2 1

In memory of
Lisa Sanders Ressell
A free-spirited daughter who brought such happiness to our family

Contents

Figures

Preface

Almost every book on decisionmaking sooner or later discusses problem solving. Some time ago I heard a funny story about the impact of problems on the human's scheme of things. It has relevance for this volume.

A dispirited man was complaining bitterly to his friend about the terrible problems that he recently had experienced. "Three weeks ago my uninsured business burned down." His friend answered, "It could have been worse." The victim next told of his wife's death two weeks earlier. Again, the response was, "It could have been worse." Finally, the troubled man blurted out, "Last week the police jailed my son for selling drugs." He heard the same answer. "It could have been worse." Very irritated the complainant shouted, "I tell you about these terrible events and all you can say is, 'It could have been worse.' Tell me, what could have been worse?" His friend answered promptly, "It could have happened to me."

In their personal and professional lives, executives inevitably experience problems. They might wish these problems would affect only others but, as we know, life does not happen that way. Consequently, it is better that executives prepare to face those problems that affect both their decisions and their decisionmaking. In this book I examine the nature of problems and decisionmaking, including the impact of both on people who direct organizations. Furthermore, this work focuses on how executives respond to problems at the upper levels of organizations.

Some of our better minds have commented on this subject. Peter Drucker aptly observed, "Only executives make decisions. The first managerial skill is, therefore, the making of effective decisions" (Drucker, 1973, p. 465). Venerable Aristotle recognized that the making of decisions constituted a prime function of government: wise decisions led to good public policy. Thus, whether in the private or in the public sector, decisionmaking plays a key role. The subject of decisionmaking, both in its practice and as a subject for academic study, has evolved in many ways during the past decades. I have had the good fortune to have taught this subject during my lifetime as a teacher and witnessed executives making important decisions during various episodes in my career.

To date the literature devoted to executive decisionmaking has consistently failed to give proper emphasis to certain important aspects. In seeking to remedy these deficiencies, this book stresses (1) problem identification, which executives frequently neglect because of their preoccupation with problem solving; (2) the need to avoid viewing solutions as remedies achieved at predetermined milestones; (3) assessing solutions in terms of the severity of problems both before and after executives try to fix them, that is, the problem exchange ratio (PER); (4) examining options in outcomes other than solutions, such as accommodating and coping; and (5) the executive environment associated with outcomes, along a spectrum ranging from perfection to progress to failure.

Some of the ideas in this volume do not appear elsewhere in today's literature. Although other books have treated other concepts discussed on these pages, by and large they have given them short shrift. In this volume, I have attempted to give these neglected notions the attention that they deserve. In so doing, I hope that I have introduced some new directions that provide "something of value." If I have, then the reader will find it worthwhile to read this book.

I attempted to bridge the gap between scholarly and practical approaches to the subject. As one of my goals, I sought to translate academic thought into practical prose. Yet in no way is this a "how-to" book. You'll find no recipes here. Nor does it dwell on minutiae or purely technical matters. Rather, it provides frames of reference and an intellectual sounding board against which practicing or aspiring executives can bounce their own ideas.

Although this book chiefly examines the actual experience associated with how executives make decisions, it still explores in a major way its conceptual aspects. In other words, this work addresses the subject from both the theoretical and practical points of view. Alone, neither would explain the subject in a satisfactory way.

I am quite aware that at times both decisions and problems tend to be "messy," unclear, and incomplete. I also understand that executives sometimes base their approach to problems and to decisions on intuition and on occasions without much, if any, conscious reasoning. However, I spent most of my time and effort examining problems and decisions from their rational perspectives because I prefer that executives use logic in conducting their business.

Having taken the aforementioned path does not mean that I have adopted wholesale a quantitative analytical approach. I have found that qualitative methods can be quite revealing and useful. However, I see the value in the former and have used it for comparing the gravity of component problems. A number of extant quantitative research techniques, not employed here, also might have a potential use in problem identification. For example, the Delphi method attempts to make effective use of informed judgments in identifying and assessing problems and issues.

This volume does not limit its discussions to the private sector. I believe that executives in the private sector suffer because they tend to focus exclusively on studying executive behavior in the business world. The responsibilities and activities of executives may change somewhat from institution to institution. Nonetheless, many of the demands on executives and how they respond remain the same regardless of the type of organization that they direct. The cases in this study illustrate the manner in which executives lead and guide a variety of institutions both private and public.

The cases and episodes in this book provide examples of how executives reacted both wisely and ineptly in addressing problems. Cases illustrating failures help readers learn from the lapses and mistakes of others; those showing success instruct them on the right way to do things. At any rate, the cases in this volume provide a series of events that readers can study to gain knowledge and insights about the art of decisionmaking. Although these cases allow them to consider concrete facts and events rather than abstractions and theories, readers can derive broad lessons and principles from the specific happenings in these cases.

Although I have stressed certain ideas that I believe add to our knowledge about decisionmaking, I also have tried to summarize briefly existing knowledge associated with these new concepts. Thus, the reader has access to both aspects of decisionmaking.

I hope this volume meets the needs of its readers. This would give me the greatest satisfaction.

Acknowledgments

No one encouraged me more in this endeavor than Dr. Peter Petersen of Johns Hopkins University. His keen observations saved me from going astray or sinning against logic, especially in the early stages of this effort. He also made it possible for me to teach a course in advances in technology and another on management science. I also owe much to the late Dr. Lowell Hattery, who arranged for me to teach courses about technology and administration at the American University. In teaching these classes, I believe that I learned as much as the students.

I also am deeply indebted to Dr. Jay Alden of the Information Resources Management College of the National Defense University (NDU) for allowing me to pick his fertile brain. Dr. Steve Knode, also of NDU, saw the need for a work emphasizing the points that I examine. They have both taught courses that bordered on this subject, and I gained from my conversations with them. Other colleagues at NDU were of great help in preparing this manuscript.

By appointing me to the J. Carlton Ward, Jr. Chair, Rear Admiral Ron Narmi, U.S. Navy, Retired, gave me the time and resources to conduct necessary research during the early phases of my project. I was flattered by being named the first faculty member at the Industrial College of the Armed Forces (ICAF) to hold that chair. Col. Joseph Muckerman, U.S. Army, Retired, colleague and close friend at the Industrial College, did much to enhance my understanding of how executives behaved in a government department. Mary Quintero and Ann Sullivan, formerly of the NDU Library, conducted literature searches and gave me sound advice about documentation. Always helpful, Susan Lemke assisted in arranging matters so that I could continue to use the NDU Library after I retired. I benefited from stimulating discussions with Dr. Dora Alves, formerly at NDU.

Dr. Robert Sigethy, Dean of the Business School at Marymount College in northern Virginia, enabled me to teach a course in public administration that helped me formulate my ideas and concepts. My son, Seth, an economist at Carnegie Mellon University, acted as a valued reviewer. He took great delight in pointing out his father's slippages in the logic of economics. More important, he contributed some trenchant criticism of my key problem exchange ratio concept and offered some sound ideas for improving it. Dr. Ashish Arora, his colleague at Carnegie Mellon, reviewed the manuscript, making valuable observations about several of my key ideas. I also had worthwhile discussions with my younger son, Ethan, who is on the staff of the American Society for Training and Development. Without his help in fixing computer failures, I would have been lost.

I am beholden to Dr. Fred Brown, who gave me wise counsel and incisive criticism. I never cease to marvel at the energy and talent that my wife, Rayleona, brings to editing my manuscripts and to discovering new ways in which to use the computer. She swept away fuzzy ideas, developed a useful index, and contributed significantly to plain and clear language.

The views expressed here are my own and reflect neither the perceptions nor the policies of the universities and other organizations in which I have worked. Although I gained from the advice of many knowledgeable people, I alone assume responsibility for any errors on these pages.

PART I

Problem Identification

CHAPTER 1

Introduction

When Arthur Whitaker taught at the University of Pennsylvania, he delighted in telling about the time that he interviewed Generalissimo Francisco Franco of Spain. Entering Franco's office, he greeted the Spanish ruler, who sat in a handsome chair behind a massive desk. Two letter boxes, one on each side of the desk, caught Whitaker's eye. The box on the left had the label "For problems that time will solve." The other box noted "For problems that time has solved." The Spanish dictator had no more to do than shift papers from the box on the left to the one on the right.

CRITICAL QUESTIONS

Time took care of problems in Franco's Spain. Whitaker's story addresses a neglected but important subject: identifying problems. Relying on the signs on his desk boxes, the Spanish leader saw no need to identify problems with precision. Unfortunately, most of us can't afford this luxury and must deal realistically with our problems. It pays us, then, to look closely into the meaning and significance of recognizing problems and how to go about addressing them. Specifically, executives must develop better insights by asking the following questions:

- Does the executive have problems?
- In recognizing problems, what kind of processes do executives use in their investigations?
- To what degree (if any) are problems caused by a failure in the internal dynamics of human performance?
- To what degree (if any) are problems caused by a failure in external conditions?
- To what degree (if any) are problems caused by a failure in the interaction between internal human performance and external environmental conditions?

This volume makes no attempt to answer the specifics of these questions. Executives in their individual organizations have to address them. Moreover, these specifics differ from organization to organization and from case to case. Yet the answers affect whether executives are focusing on the correct concerns. To help readers gain a clearer perception of this matter, this chapter opens by briefly discussing two cases:

- "Failure in School" discusses a problem that sometimes plagues parents whose children find the early school years difficult.
- "Project Mohole" discusses a problem that public officials met in fashioning a strategy and an effective organization for starting up a new activity that has scientific goals.

Failure in School

Throughout his school days our younger son experienced great difficulty in reading aloud and in writing legibly. At first, his mother and I thought that he was just a very active boy. He seemed unable to sit still, and he had a short attention span. He became irritated or seemed bored in school. Spelling gave him fits. In fact, he often spelled the same word differently several times on a page and spelled it wrong each time. Often he would read words and write them in reverse sequence. He resisted any attempts to get him to read aloud in class. Also, no one could decipher his handwriting, and his teachers must have shuddered when they tried to read what he had written. His arithmetic, too, left much to be desired. His overall performance was poor, and he thought he was dumb.

Not only did my son's academic performance suffer, but he behaved poorly in class. His teachers believed that he did not perform as well as he could have and complained about his inability to see a task through to its completion. Sometimes, he played pranks in class. More often, he withdrew from the scene and daydreamed. Some of his teachers thought him simply dumb, lazy, and disruptive. Others reasoned that emotional disabilities kept him from being a competent student. Still others reported that my son was a spoiled child living in a permissive family that never exacted the necessary discipline to help him to succeed in school. His teachers suggested that we should punish him by denying him pleasures until he improved his academic performance and classroom behavior.

My wife and I had little talent for punishment, so we consulted a highly recommended child psychologist and learning specialist. She held no pre-conceived notions about his difficulties. She gave my son a series of standardized tests. After analyzing the results, she concluded that my son suffered from an ailment known as dyslexia. His teachers had identified the wrong problem, and consequently, they applied solutions that, although they seemed logical and reasonable to them, failed to remedy the difficulty.

Dyslexia is a chronic disorder that inhibits a person's ability to recognize and process symbols, particularly those associated with language. The psychologist saw it as the cause for his poor school pattern. Our son's inadequate skills and atrocious handwriting resulted from the same disorder. The child needed specialized learning techniques, not increasingly firmer discipline.

Evidence exists for a genetic cause for this dysfunction. It often runs in families. As the psychologist noted the difficulties that plagued my son, I turned to my wife and blurted out, "Those are the same problems I had when I was his age." Also, in the spring of 1995 I had a talk with my nephew, a well-known television reporter. He had covered such events as the Persian Gulf War and the U.S. invasion of Haiti. As I told him of my dyslexia, he responded that he suffered from the same ailment, which prompted him to become a television journalist rather than a newspaper reporter. In TV he did not have to worry about his handwriting.

The psychologist also told us that although certain new learning techniques give promise of improving our son's skills, we should not expect all his difficulties to disappear. Problems conceivably might persist into adulthood. This proved true for my son. Once he knew that he had the ability to learn, that he wasn't stupid, he was able to progress by working differently than his classmates. Happily, teaching him through methods that overrode his disability led to a very successful college experience. After college, he became a very competent professional.

Today, most likely, teachers would not make this mistake. They no longer seem committed to believing that emotional disabilities cause all reading and handwriting problems. Almost all enlightened educators today recognize dyslexia and can recommend help.

Project Mohole

In 1957 the American Miscellaneous Society (AMSOC), an informal gathering of highly qualified American scientists, proposed that the United States drill a hole through the crust of the earth to the Mohorvic Discontinuity. They called this effort "Project Mohole" (U.S. House, 1969). These scientists aimed to gather geological knowledge about "inner space," just as the National Aeronautics and Space Administration (NASA) collected information about "outer space." AMSOC took responsibility for managing the Mohole program and designed and conducted experiments. It eventually contracted with an industrial firm to build a platform from which to drill the hole.

These scientists argued that, just as in the space program, the United States engaged in a race with the Soviets for discovering new and important facts about the earth's geology. The National Science Foundation (NSF) agreed to fund this endeavor.

Nine years later, some congressmen called the project a giant boondoggle and scrapped it. The project had run into several major difficulties, technical and otherwise; its executives seemed unsure if they next should drill several small holes or one big hole. Some informed observers suggested that costs would swell to half a billion dollars over the next 20 to 30 years.

In this case, AMSOC and NSF failed to determine exactly the kind of problem that confronted them. At the outset, AMSOC scientists should have asked: "Above all, how difficult would it be to gain the knowledge needed to build a technology capable of digging into the depths of the earth?" "Can the United States realistically conduct such a major engineering project?" "Would such a project improve the technological and scientific position of the United States in a meaningful, cost-effective way?" "Does the country really need such a vast increase in geological information?" "Can AMSOC realistically expect the nation to supply the amounts and kinds of resources necessary for such a project, including vast finances, scientific knowledge, technological managerial competence, talent, and training capacity?" "How can the nation best allocate resources among the various aspects of the project?" "Should AMSOC confine all resources to digging the large hole to the mantle, or should some interim digging be undertaken first?"

Instead of focusing on these relevant questions, AMSOC scientists seem to have addressed less important problems: "Can ocean and geological science improve the nation's image?" "Can AMSOC scientists capture a necessary share of the nation's research and development resources?" "Can U.S. science beat Soviet science in this important field?" "How can AMSOC, as originator of this project, secure a future for its scientists and retain its dominant leadership position?" If these scientists had asked the right questions initially, they would have been in a better position to try to solve the right problem. They could have been more selective about the information that they used.

Certainly by discovering new fundamental knowledge about this earth, scientists could improve their idea of the nature of planet Earth and the universe. The project also probably would discover some practical knowledge that would prove useful in the here and now.

Above all, AMSOC scientists failed to inquire whether Project Mohole chiefly posed a scientific or a technological challenge. As they became more deeply immersed in the project, they must have seen that to an overwhelming degree the task became technological. The project executives found the engineering tasks more demanding of their time and attention.

The project never did reach the major (scientific) geological information-gathering stage. Throughout its life, the project expended its main effort toward engineering tasks. It had to build the machine that would later enable scientists to unearth new knowledge. If AMSOC's executives had examined NASA's Apollo Project, they would have recognized that most resources went into technological activities. Consequently, AMSOC did not select appropriate decisionmaking options. For example, unlike NASA, it chose to administer the program through scientists rather than through professional managers who also had extensive engineering experience. Likewise, at the outset, it failed to assemble the hardware needed for an undertaking of this sort.

American philosopher John Dewey would have faulted AMSOC for failing to address adequately his first step in problem solving: "What is the problem?" (Dewey, 1910). Because AMSOC executives did not target the right problem at the outset, the project eventually failed.

WHAT IS A PROBLEM?

Quite a number of authors have contributed insightful observations about the subject of problems. For example, Herbert Simon (1957) has added useful knowledge about the psychology of problems as they relate to decisionmaking. Some other recent major contributors include Peter Drucker (1974), Russell Ackoff (1978), Stephen Andriole (1983), and Charles Margerison (1974). Some observers—William Gruber and John Niles, for instance—assert that the problems confronting leaders in business, government, universities, and other institutions were more serious during the 1970s and 1980s than they had been in the past (1976, p. x). Thus, one can conclude that problems demanded more attention during those decades.

Yet the executive must begin with a sound idea of what constitutes a problem. It should come as no surprise that over the years the word *problem* has accumulated several definitions in the literature. In large part, definitions of problems contain within them the act of problem solving. As its first and preferred definition, the *American Heritage Dictionary of the English Language* (1992) looks at a problem as "a question to be considered, solved or answered." The *Shorter Oxford University*

Dictionary (1989) likewise labels it as "a difficult question posed for a solution." Fred Brown uses almost these very words in defining a problem (1977, p. 92). McGuire and Putzell suggest, "An annual employee turnover rate of 25 percent is not a problem, but simply a given. It becomes a problem only when someone finds a way to reduce it; that is, a solution" (1989, p. 258). All these definitions highlight the idea that one can think of problems in terms of something being solved (Robertshaw, Mecca, and Rerick, 1978).

A more appropriate perspective views a problem as a discrepancy—an inconsistency between two phenomena that should be in accord. Discrepancies exist between (1) what is and what is not happening, (2) what is expected and what is the reality, (3) what is desired and what is achieved, (4) what is in one's interests or in the interests of competitors, enemies, allies, or just others, and (5) the need to convince others as to the validity of problems. Let's look at each of these in turn.

First, when considering problems as a gap between what is and what is not occurring, one can benefit from consulting John Arnold. He rightfully suggests that instead of asking, "What is a problem?" one should ask, "What is happening that should be happening or what is happening that should not be happening?" (1992, p. 12). Any situation in which a gap exists between what is and what is not might present a problem (Van Gundy, 1981, p. 3).

Said another way, all problems share a common characteristic—dissatisfaction with what exists. Modern executives would gain by using the word *problem* chiefly as meaning *dissatisfaction with administrative performance.* For example, when the first U.S.-made rocket, the Vanguard, blew up on the launching pad, almost everyone blamed the fiasco on the project's administrators (who else?). In this connection, the important point to remember is that executives should remain sensitive to indicators that show a dissatisfaction with a situation.

Second, Jay Alden (1997) gives us another useful slant. Executives naturally have expectations of what the future might bring. At the same time, decisionmakers must live in a real world in which they observe and measure performance. Executives often face the task of examining the relationship between expectations and reality by processing information. When they find discrepancies between the two, they discover problems.

For example, peasants in underdeveloped societies live with poverty and experience dull lives. They cannot make life more comfortable and interesting. Once exposed to some economic and technological development, they exhibit the well-known "revolution of rising expectations." They become dissatisfied with poverty and monotony, often without knowing how to escape. This kind of revolution has led to turbulence and armed conflict in societies.

On the other hand, many people in the developed world increasingly complain about what industrialization has done to their environment. Many Americans look at the filthy rivers, dirty air, dangerous land fills, and strip mines and long for the beauty of the land before "progress" sullied it. The great success and influence of Rachel Carson's *Silent Spring* (1962), which bemoaned what toxins like DDT had done to the environment, speak eloquently of how deeply this feeling runs within people.

Third, a difference exists between how much decisionmakers attain and what they desire. Donald C. Gause and Gerald M. Weinberg (1982) contend that a problem is the difference between things as desired and things as perceived. They can consider not meeting their expectations a problem, and yet they might not want to meet those expectations. For example, as a general rule employees might want executives to supervise closely and fairly the rules for taking sick leave (otherwise the firm might face the problem of increased personnel costs to their detriment), but they do not wish that bosses severely limit the types of situations for which they might grant such leave.

The point noted here relates to the tendency of executives to look at problems as the difference between what they perceive as reality and what they prefer reality to be. In other words, one also can define the word *problem* as a disparity between what actually exists and what humans desire. Eden, Jones, and Sims echo this same perspective and take it one step further, stating, "We usually refer to ourselves as having a problem if things are not what we would like them to be [worth] and we are not quite sure what to do about it" (1983, p. 12).

Fourth, noted philosopher William James (1990, pp. 668–671) sensibly pointed out that people can define a problem according to their own interests. The statesman thinks and acts in terms of interest defined as the power of the state, whereas the chief executive officer (CEO) defines that interest in terms of directing a profitable company. Put another way, the nature of that interest arises from the relationship between the goals of executives and the realities of their circumstances. Some executives, sensitive to human reactions to unsatisfactory conditions, prefer to use such euphemisms as "opportunities" or "challenges" rather than "problems"; even if executives or organizations do view a given situation as an opportunity, they still tend to see that opportunity in terms of protecting or enhancing their interests.

Fifth, discrepancies must convince differing elements within an organization that a problem exists. After all, those who discover problems have to persuade others, who might have disparate ideas about conditions, to agree to their findings. Thus, the rhetoric of definitions becomes very important because definitions have to be communicated within institutions. Others have to understand them in order to agree to them. Above all, definitions require a rhetoric that shows the link between the definition and the interests of the organization (McGuire and Putzell, 1989). Thus, in addressing a problem, the principal aim of the executive is to remove the discrepancy or to fill the gap.

The Executive's Role

In addressing the nature of problems, executives naturally have to remember their responsibilities in directing organizations. They have to perform the functions of deliberate control, management, supervision, and administration. Consequently, in the public sector we traditionally think of top executives as those who direct the total government bureaucracy. For a long time, observers and scholars have used this tag to label the branches of government that historically execute the laws passed by legislatures. Executives also long have been used in business to designate people who carry on certain responsibilities in large business enterprises. In the past six or seven decades, sociologists have studied these individuals and their functions in great detail, giving us new insights into how those at the top view unwanted situations (Bernard, 1968). Whether conscious of it or not, their supervisors rate the performance of executives in part on how well they understand the nature of problems.

PROBLEM IDENTIFICATION VS. PROBLEM SOLVING

In order to compensate for the lack of attention that the literature gives to the executive's task of finding problems before setting out to remedy them, it is necessary to sharpen the distinction between problem finding and problem solving. At the outset, however, we have to acknowledge that most authors understand the need for defining what a problem is in the first place. For example, in their comprehensive textbook on decision-making, Kleindorfer, Kunreuther, and Schoemaker state, "At issue is not only how decision makers 'solve problems,' but also how they came to identify and accept such problems and learn from the results of their actions" (1993, p. 3).

In other words, one should find out what is wrong before trying to do anything about it. If executives took this advice seriously, they would run less risk of being disappointed. Yet in real life, all too often those in charge attempt to solve problems before identifying them with a precision that ensures that they are on the right course. Placing most of one's efforts first to solving problems brings to mind the age-old saying about putting the cart before the horse.

Put another way, executives owe it to their profession not to allow their diagnostic thinking to be brought prematurely to a close by not identifying problems sufficiently before rushing into solutions.

Consequently, Part I of this book contains one overridding message: *All too often, executives fashion excellent solutions for the wrong problems.* Ian

Mitroff (1998) sees the business community committing this fault over and over and making situations worse instead of better. Often the assumptions and premises that executives make about the nature of the problem prove incorrect (Picken and Dess, 1998, p. 42). At all costs, executives should guard against expending considerable resources trying to solve problems that do not exist (Adams, 1979, pp. 7–11) or that exist in a way not clearly formulated in the executive's mind.

Scholars also suggest that "the problem or decision situation is linked to potential improvements that may be achievable" (Kleindorfer, Kunreuther, and Schoemaker, 1993, p. 25). In making this assertion they infer that problem identification, too, has a problem-solving aspect to it, arguing, "Problem identification is the process by which a decisionmaker recognizes that a problem or decision-making opportunity exists" (p. 24). This book parts company with such traditional thinking. It questions the common practice of including aspects of problem solving within the definition of problems (Albert, 1980; King, 1981). Whether improvements are achievable has nothing to do with the existence of a problem. Definitions of a problem should not include this idea. Problems would exist even if no advances were achievable. All a problem needs is dissatisfaction with what is or what should be. These authors also include the criteria for resolving the problem within problem identification, another concept that I have trouble accepting. I suggest that criteria for resolving problems belong to the task of solving problems and not identifying them.

In finding problems, executives must discover more than facts and resources. They also must unearth why organizations fumble. For example, why did organizations provide inappropriate resources (people, information, technology, money, or materiel) (Schoennauer, 1981, p. 16)? This task leads them to look for values and beliefs that undergird the wrong actions.

On the other hand, these textbook writers do aptly define problem solving in a straightforward way. They maintain that "[p]roblem solving is the activity associated with taking action or choice so as to resolve well-formulated problems" (Kleindorfer, Kunreuther, and Schoemaker, 1993, p. 10). They understand that the task of choosing and assessing alternatives and then determining which one is best or most appropriate lies at the heart of problem solving. One should note that although executives stand a better chance of selecting the right option if the problem is well formulated, by applying sound reasoning they probably still have an opportunity to do so even if the problem is not expressed in the best way possible.

Let us look at the proper perspective of the two concepts as suggested by Schoennauer: "Problem-finding capability is that of a sleuth, discovering and piecing together past events; problem-solving anticipates the consequences and implications of a contemplated course of action" (1981,

p. 16). Notice that this author rightly makes a sharp distinction between the two.

IMPORTANCE OF PHRASING

In discussing the essence of problems, one cannot overstate the importance of precision in phrasing the questions that executives fashion to discover adverse occurrences. One kind of wording rather than another could describe a set of conditions in very different ways. Even the use of a single word can make a big difference. Let's look at two statements: "Top executives 'could' not rely on their staffs to utilize delegated authority properly" versus "Top executives 'would' not rely on their staffs to utilize delegated authority properly."

The word *could* refers to an inability of the staffs to perform the delegated functions, even if they had the will to perform them. The word *would* conveys the idea of willingness rather than of ability. A problem statement conceivably might use both words. For example, "If the staff 'would' only try to use delegated authority, it 'could' perform its mission in an outstanding way." Each of the preceding two problem statements calls for a different solution. In responding to the word *would*, top executives might try to provide staffs with more incentives, encouraging them to perform this function enthusiastically; they might promise promotions or larger salaries. In the case of *could*, they might provide staffs with more resources (e.g., additional people) or additional training to improve their ability to handle delegated authority.

FINDING INFORMATION

In order to discover a problem, executives must become aware of the information in which it appears. To gain such cognizance, they have to understand how to conduct inquiries, a demanding task by any standard. Yet executives only can comprehend the nature and dynamics of their own continuing development by gaining a deeper understanding of how to use an information base. The term *information* relates to facts and opinions in words and numbers contained in sources, often called "data bases" (Hartwig and Dearing, 1979). Executives can use this process for transforming unconnected items in a raw information base into recognized problems.

Figure 1.1 displays this process. It reflects the flow of thought that decisionmakers generally apply in recognizing unsatisfactory conditions. Figure 1.1 represents one major way of coming to grips with the task of identifying problems.

At the top level of the information process, decisionmakers attempt to translate their experiences in the real world into meaningful words and

Figure 1.1
Problem Identification Process

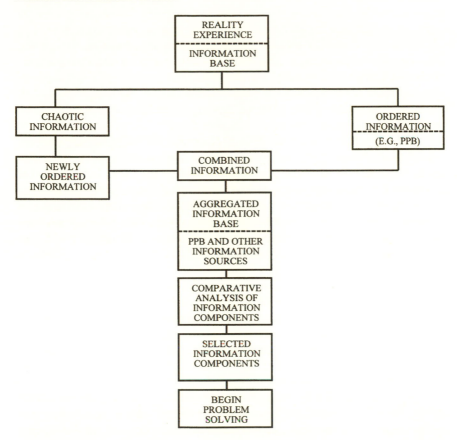

numbers that depict the essence of this reality. They store this information in what we call an "information base." In doing their jobs, executives extract from the information base the facts, ideas, and notions that make up real problems.

On the second level, decisionmakers discover that information usually appears in one of two conditions. In the block on the right, one finds well-ordered information. Documents containing this type of data include, among others, corporate strategies, accounting sources, profit and loss statements, cash flow statements, environmental quality reports, productivity studies, program evaluation and review technique (PERT) reports, and plans, programs, and budgets (PPBs). (See Chapter 4 for a discussion of PPBs.)

Simultaneously, on this level executives can run into chaotic situations. In the block on the left appear items of information that do not seem logically connected. Most often this condition exists when one deals with raw data that have not been processed, edited, interpreted, or prepared into a useful form. Obviously, working with chaotic information poses a more demanding challenge than dealing with well-ordered information. At this stage (third level), decisionmakers have to use vigorous systematic thinking when attempting to transform the chaos into an ordered structure (such as a company's financial statement).

If necessary, executives link new information with existing well-organized data (level 3) to produce aggregated information (level 4), including all available information in usable form.

Once analysts have aggregated and classified the information, they try to come up with sensible components. Each component represents an individual problem. They join facts and numbers that seem to go together and separate those that seem to have no logical connection. Executives then compare information components of the current base with those of the past (level 5). They then look for linkages within the information base (level 6) and compare alternate items of information. If all goes well, executives should be able to identify an array of problems susceptible to problem-solving analysis.

The comparison of alternative information components represents the single most critical step in problem identification, just as the comparison of alternative courses of action serves in problem solving. At this stage executives take the important step of prioritizing information components that reflect problems. Only by finding the likenesses and differences in these components and estimating the most likely results can decisionmakers properly begin the problem-solving phase.

I do not argue that by using the information process decisionmakers always can come up with recognizable problems. Yet, at times, by comparing items of information, executives can come up with problems that demand attention. It would seem, then, that the problem identification process contributes a valuable way of thinking.

Sometimes this task proves difficult for decisionmakers. They sometimes lack specific directions for putting this information together. They frequently resort to implicit rather than explicit assumptions, thereby decreasing the confidence that they can have in the validity of their information.

In the final block (level 7), decisionmakers begin the process of comparing courses of action with the intent of solving problems or making the adjustment to live with them.

MAJOR DIMENSIONS

With this background in mind, the reader profits from observing the following dimensions that influence the ultimate picture of a world of problems:

1. Identity—What exactly are the characteristics of a situation that make it unsatisfactory?

2. Substance—What material things existing in the physical world cause adverse conditions?

3. Concepts—What notions and ideas do people associate with problems?

4. Participants—Who takes part in unfolding events or in the decisionmaking process?

5. Location—Where within the information base do we observe a problem?

6. Timing—When does the problem occur, and how long does it last?

7. Importance—How much influence do problems have on the way people think and behave?

8. Severity—How big is the adverse impact of a problem?

USE OF INTUITION

One should note another important point in this discussion. Sometimes one gains an impression that executives need not use analysis in discovering problems but instead could rely on intuition. Sometimes intuition works. Most of the time, nothing can be further from the truth. If observers imply that executives usually can identify problems without the conscious use of reasoning, they mislead themselves. Intuition often proves a weak device for discovering reality. Therefore, if executives simply assume that they know what a problem is and proceed to solve it, they stand a good chance of arriving at inadequate remedies.

Kleindorfer, Kurreuther, and Schoemaker seem to ask the right question in this regard: "Does the person prefer a systematic or an intuitive approach to judgment?" (1993, p. 203). More and more the literature tends to treat problems as they relate to decisionmaking as a "system" (Rerick, 1978; Robertshaw, Mecca, and Rerick, 1978). Increasingly executives are being called on to think in terms of systems when choosing among options in order to achieve goals. It is said that executives can direct an organization most effectively by considering it an organic whole with all elements logically related to each other. Although systems thought has contributed much to our understanding of decisionmaking, the chief messages of this volume do not necessarily evolve from or rely on the systems approach. In real life, some systems structures have been very successful, whereas others have failed (Drucker, 1973, pp. 592–598). One can gain useful knowledge and insights from the main points in this study without considering how relevant the systems approach is to our subject.

SPECIFIC ERRORS

At this point in the discussion, it pays to take a close look at problem identification in terms of discovering items in the information base that individually tell the executive what might or could be wrong. All too often executives tend to emphasize the whole rather than examine the parts. By stressing the whole, some authors emphasize the need to begin by interrogating a "frame of reference." These frames of reference are composed of dynamic and static assumptions, premises, beliefs, and anticipated choices (Beach and Mitchell, 1978; Mintz et al., 1997; Picken and Dess, 1998; Prahalad and Bettis, 1986; Smirchich and Stubbart, 1985). They are influenced by such factors as the motivation, the social psychology, and the personality of the executives trying to solve the problem. Although this approach might prove productive, it also could cause errors in an executive's thinking (Zahra and Chaples, 1993; Zajac and Bazerman, 1991).

In addition to the whole, executives also should pay great attention to its separate components. They would do well to examine individual parts before they put them together and then express a theory. By suggesting that the nature of problems always stems from "invalid theories" instead of from specific incorrect happenings, they find it difficult to achieve sound direction and guidance. What's more, those who study the tendency to solve the wrong problem would profit by avoiding the tendency always to express these parts in scholarly jargon. Instead, they might cite, as much as possible, the essential facts that indicate unwelcomed situations in simple language.

In this regard businesspeople or public officials can identify five categories of error: (1) identifying wrong facts that get in the way of effective operations; (2) interpreting right facts incorrectly; (3) assigning right facts to wrong environments, or vice versa; (4) giving improper weights to right or wrong facts; and (5) drawing the scope of a problem either too narrowly (Mitroff, 1998) or too broadly.

When department heads discover sales personnel taking too many breaks, they know that this fact is wrong for the proper functioning of their department. If they conclude that the initiative of certain sales personnel, while increasing sales, makes others jealous and thus bosses should discourage such enterprise, they are making an unsound interpretation of a right fact. If they place a person with no sales competence but with an ability to wrap packages in a selling position, they are assigning a right fact (technical competence in wrapping) to a wrong environment. If they place an individual with little selling ability in a department needing more sales personnel, they are putting the wrong fact with the right environment.

If department heads put great confidence in a salesperson's ability to speak incessantly, they are putting great weight on a wrong fact, or if they don't take advantage of their selling staff's ability to convince customers of the worth of their products, they are placing insufficient weight on the right fact. Finally, if they go deeply into the home life of sales personnel to explain poor performance, they probably have drawn too wide a scope in their investigation. Conversely, if they consider only a person's sense of humor, the scope is too narrow. In all these instances, department heads are looking at how they should relate to problems.

One additional note: In the matter of the right remedy for the wrong problem, executives also have to be aware that at times a well-known satirical proposition might influence their ability to target the problem, namely, "Murphy's Law": "If there is a possibility for something to go wrong, it will go wrong." Thus, through no fault of their own, sometimes executives encounter unanticipated, moving targets.

USE OF TECHNIQUES

Over the years, some very good minds have fashioned a cornucopia from which have tumbled a large number of rigorous techniques for analyzing problems. Successive thinkers have added new—and at times more effective, analytical, and especially quantitative—approaches to decision-making. New professions have developed and applied these new methods, specifically operations research and systems analysis. However, overwhelmingly they have designed these techniques to assist executives in comparing alternative courses of action, the core function in solving problems. As yet, analysts have made little use of systems analysis and operations research techniques in comparing alternative components of the information base.

Since the latter years of the nineteenth century, book after book seems to discover the techniques that rational decisionmakers need to guess the inadequacies of their performance. Kepner and Tregoe (1981, p. 73) make this point explicitly. The number of contributors to operations research and systems analysis has risen impressively. Despite the major growth in analytical techniques, at times executives and analysts continue to mismatch analytical methods and problems. They apply the wrong technique to the right problem, or vice versa.

In a way, planning, programming, and budgeting represent instruments leading to a kind of problem identification. In coming up with programs, executives must set the limits on the information that they use. For example, programs tell managers responsible for maintaining trucks in good shape to keep these vehicles above or below a certain weight and load capacity. They usually end up analyzing one group of trucks differently from those having dissimilar characteristics. Yet by stipulating a family of trucks having the same or similar dimensions, the analyst can identify deficiencies.

Conceptually, little or no difference exists between the information base, as used here, and management information systems. An extensive literature treats the subject of information management. Perhaps the most commonly used device for analyzing the components of an information base is applying priorities or rankings. Chapter 8 treats this subject in depth.

FEEDBACK DYNAMICS

In their efforts to identify problems, competent executives have to understand the reciprocal nature between what they put into their search for information and the amount and quality of the information that they retrieve. Analysts term this concept a "cybernetic snapshot."

It is well known that executives have long used models in seeking to explain the complexities of reality. In our model, the essence of cybernetics is the feedback that takes place between inputs and outputs through processing. How many answers and what kind of results executives gain are measured against the resources that they have to invest in their inquiries. Although cybernetics usually pertains to various mechanical, electrical, and biological systems, as used here it deals chiefly with information processing.

Figure 1.2 depicts the cybernetics model related to identifying problems. The three items at the top depict environmental factors that affect the ability of an organization to identify problems.

On the left are pictured two types of inputs: (1) the status of the data (chaotic or ordered) and (2) the types of documents within which these data appear. These sources can vary widely, and those noted in Figure 1.2 represent only a fraction of the information sources.

In the middle box executives subject the information gathered in the base to analysis in their quest to identify real and important problems. One also could call this action "the interrogation and analysis" phase.

By comparing items within the information base, joining some and separating others, analysts discover facts and data that illuminate pertinent similarities and differences, surfacing real and important problems. At a cost, identification analysis converts extant information into recognizable problems (or if the analysis is faulty, fails to convert it). The third box contains specific problems that flow from the analysis.

The key to this model, however, lies at the bottom of Figure 1.2, the feedback. Here we see that outputs, in turn, alter the original inputs, triggering another round of analysis. In other words, part of the output feeds back into the system as new inputs that analysts can use in identifying subsequent problems.

Certain prejudices prevent decisionmakers from profiting from proper feedback. Russo and Schoemaker (1989, pp. 176–187) cite three: (1) a desire to claim credit for success, (2) a desire to rationalize away mistakes, and (3) the distorting effects of hindsight on memory. One could add a

Figure 1.2
Cybernetics Model: Process of Problem Identification

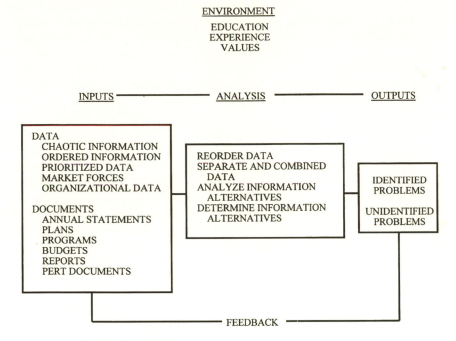

fourth, the absence of a logical process for making comparisons. To the degree that decisionmakers are unwilling to discard the first three biases and to establish a well-thought-through process for conducting analyses, they will continue to take greater risks in selecting which problems they determine they have to address.

COMMUNICATIONS

No matter how effectively an executive assesses problems, an inability to communicate one's thoughts to others within an organization impedes, in a major way, a person's ability to get rid of unwanted conditions. After all, communications acts as a linking process within complex systems such as private firms or government agencies. Executives must acquire or have available to them basic communication skills for letting others know what is wrong and what they intend to do about it. The aforementioned cybernetics model depends upon communications. In fact, to the practicing executive, cybernetics may appear to have little value other than to reinforce the need for communication feedback (F. Brown, 1977, p. 31).

SUMMARY

Problems are defined as dissatisfaction with things as they are. However, a need for the right solution always remains. If decisionmakers fail initially to become aware of the right problem, they later tend to choose the wrong courses of action. Should that situation take place, effective decisionmaking is not possible. Executives have available to them guidance frameworks that should help them identify problems. They have many techniques for solving problems but few for identifying them. A number of scholars examining this question have contributed a variety of approaches. People have paid varying amounts of attention to problem solving and have come to understand that the information process has a cybernetic quality. Executives also should have the ability to communicate their ideas and concepts clearly to others within the institution. In addition, the cybernetics model rests on effective communications.

It pays to reiterate here a key sentence that pertains to the entire first part of this volume: *All too often, executives fashion excellent solutions for the wrong problems.* As a matter of course, they should take care to avoid the pitfall of ignoring problem identification. To do so requires that executives pay special attention to this fault.

CHAPTER 2

Doing the Job

Without doubt, an executive who has a good understanding of the dynamics of the job will be more likely to do the job well. This statement might seem obvious and not worth noting here, yet one will profit by keeping it in mind. Executives can find themselves in deep trouble if they forget this obvious advice.

THE LOGIC OF DECISIONMAKING

Before discussing the logic of decisionmaking, it is good to point out a well-known fact: In real life, decisionmaking is a highly political process, sometimes requiring executives to form coalitions in order to convert decisions into actualities. The commonly held belief that executives get their work done through others rings true. Although it is correct that in dealing with others on occasion effective executives have to exercise power, most of the time they have to try to achieve consensus or, at least, try to gain the approval of as many people as possible. Moreover, most often they attempt to get their way through influence and winning cooperation rather than by commanding others to bend to their wills. The aspect of decisionmaking devoted to requiring approvals and authorizations of many different people on various levels of the organization has been treated elsewhere in the literature (Yukl, 1994, pp. 448–451) and needs no elaboration here.

We all know that knowledge gives the executive power. Gary Yukl correctly points out that "[t]he control over important information is a major source of power in organizations" (p. 448). A top executive's sole possession of or access to information makes subordinates rely more on the executive to find out what is happening in their organization.

The discussion in this book examines chiefly one aspect of decision-making—the logical approach that executives have to employ most of the time in eliminating disagreeable situations.

In making decisions, executives should try to consider all alternate paths from the initial state of unwanted conditions to the state of achieved goals (March, 1994). Yet we cannot always assume that executives want to make a decision, even if one seems called for (Alden, 1997) (although one can conclude that the act of not making a decision is in itself a decision). However, making decisions remains a prime duty of executives, and those unwilling to make them usually fade from the scene.

In thinking about the role that problem identification plays in decision-making, executives should be willing to think beyond their "comfort thresholds," that is, beyond the point at which they find discovery easy. Logic leads operators first to survey the information pool. Then they divide, aggregate, and arrange that information into some logical pattern. The question next arises, "What priorities should executives set on the various items of information that they have discovered?" In determining whether to build a new industry in a community, entrepreneurs certainly have to consider more than the specifications, cost, and production and distribution schedule associated with its products. They have to consider broader economic and ecological problems. For instance, they have to take into account the dimensions of the inimicable consequences of the pollution that new industries produce.

Frank Harrison (1987, p. 5) suggests that a tendency exists in the real world to view decisionmaking and problem solving as twins; the terms are often used interchangeably. Harrison aptly stresses that these words are not synonymous. Problem solving constitutes a component of decision-making, usually referring to that part related to the act of applying resources. Russell Ackoff (1978) advances the theme that problem solving, in large part, relates to the state of one's relevant ideas.

AWARENESS

Executives naturally face the formidable demand of becoming aware of conditions around them, especially about conditions that really bother them. Some tend to choose the easiest solution suggested by the facts they find. Nowhere does one see this tendency acted out with more audacity (and humor) than in the following story.

While transporting mental patients, a bus driver stopped at a roadside stand for a few beers. When he returned to his bus, it was empty. The 20 patients had disappeared. Realizing the trouble he was in, he stopped his bus at the next bus stop and offered lifts to those in the queue. Letting 20 people board, he shut the doors and drove straight to the mental hospital, where he hastily handed over his "charges," warning the nurse that this load of "patients" was particularly excitable. The staff took the furious passengers to the wards. Three days later, hospital administrators, made suspicious by the consistency of stories that these new "patients" told, set them free. As for the mental patients who had escaped, nothing more was heard from them, and they apparently blended comfortably back into society.

If modern executives behaved like this bus driver, our institutions would collapse. The easiest solution may not be the best. Executives require the talent and the training to identify when someone tries to foist "bogus patients" on them. They should have the skill and determination to find the "mental patients" that got away. That task may be formidable, but for the good of their institutions, modern bosses must meet such challenges.

As with all human endeavors, to investigate an information base successfully requires more than innate ability; it demands properly trained and dynamic executives (Driver, Brousseau, and Hunsaker, 1993, pp. 451–509). After all, by taking action, executives often seek to perform the difficult task of changing the traditional ways in which institutions act. For the purposes of this study, no need exists to examine this subject in depth. It is enough to say that by staying alert executives can gain knowledge about something gone wrong. For example, farmers really get to know the true meaning of mayhem when a fox gets into the chicken coop.

In a very practical way, no unwanted or unsatisfactory situation exists unless the human mind "seizes" it. As noted earlier, before people can become aware that a problem exists, they must become dissatisfied with an actual situation (Grove, 1983). This is the starting point at which executives and analysts begin their investigations.

To repeat the key point discussed here, we know that the human mind can become aware that a problem exists. At times and under certain conditions, a community shares this knowledge. As long as homosexuals and drug addicts were the major populations suffering from AIDS (acquired immunodeficiency syndrome), the American people were largely unaware of and paid little attention to the disease. When thousands of individuals from various walks of life (especially from the middle classes) were found to be HIV positive, the public increasingly recognized the illness as a major health problem.

COGNITION

Closely related to awareness is cognition. In simple terms, cognition is the act of knowing. In its cognitive mode, the human mind resembles an information-processing instrument (Wallsten, 1980). The mind works by absorbing knowledge from various sources of information (Arkes and Hammond, 1986). What's more, the design of a problem can be studied as a cognitive activity (Hinrichs, 1992, pp. 6–7). Swiss psychologist Jean Piaget ("Piaget, Jean," 1990) noted that when knowledge contradicts tradition, people suffer what he called "cognitive dissonance." This fact is interesting to this study, which points out that tension and conflict (dissonance) often afflict people, leading them to warp reality. Cognitive dissonance brings to the attention of people that anxieties exist (hence, problems) (Axelrod, 1976). For the purposes of this volume, we need not here explore in depth the growing literature on this subject.

As might be expected, cognition suffers from some widely recognized limitations. Both human cognitive biases and imperfect communications systems at times make it difficult for the executive to recognize that a problem exists. In addition, because cognition acts as a human computer, it suffers some of the same frailties as that machine. Memory, a key element in both cognition and computers, can fail. As we know, information storage mechanisms have deficiencies. Nonetheless, those seeking a fuller understanding of problem identification must comprehend how cognition enables people to gain a realistic picture of unwanted conditions.

THE CREATIVE ACT

We recognize that executives can identify problems more effectively by thinking creatively (Moore, 1958; Osborn, 1949; Parnes and Harding, 1962). At times they require creativity in order to survive. For example, we know that to maintain themselves in the global marketplace U.S. companies had to fashion new and improved commercial opportunities at a more rapid rate than their rivals (Oden, 1997).

We generally define *creativity* as the ability to produce something new or as intellectual inventiveness. The most important characteristic of the creative process is originality (uniqueness). We hope that something "new" also offers something beneficial. Hickman and Silva suggest a key aspect of creativity for executives, namely, that when as a matter of course they look at things differently they see their creativity grow naturally (1984, p. 113).

Why is creative thought so important in identifying problems? The answer is straightforward. Those interrogating an information base usually work within the confines of known facts. Executives often examine such subjects as production, inventories, maintenance, operations, attitudes, jobs, institutions, and interpersonal relationships. Yet we all know that the information base can seem complex and unclear. What's more, executives often operate with closed minds, burdened with preconceived viewpoints and unwilling to go beyond previous boundaries of thought. Put another way, some executives tend to think within existing intellectual boxes, reluctant to break out into new territory. Every creative act passes beyond the established order in some way. At times, decisionmakers have difficulty seeing what is wrong or discovering new solutions (new possibilities) until they depart from the familiar and find unanticipated significant relationships within the information base.

Working with known facts, the creative mind, by some leap of the imagination, develops novel combinations and ideas (Sanders, 1975, pp. 9–11). By observing pertinent similarities and differences within the information base, the creative mind discovers new situations. By using unconventional thought, analysts hope to make visible previously hidden unsatisfactory situations. They attempt to contribute new thought by perceiving unexpected and important departures from generally accepted ideas (Steiner, 1965). Above all, identifying problems requires as much creative effort as solving them.

We also know that creativity, including that which bosses apply in discovering problems, is not entirely an intellectual effort. More often than not, it relies on highly personal factors. For example, successful executives usually exhibit an intense commitment to unearthing hidden problems.

Head Ski Company, Inc.

Entrepreneurs know full well that being creative helps them overcome problems and establish new, advantageous frontiers. In the late 1940s, Howard Head detected a key problem preventing the growth of skiing as a major sport. At that time, most American skiers bought imported wooden skis. Head, an experienced aircraft designer, spent more than three years developing a metal ski that would not break, turned easily, and tracked correctly without shimmying and chattering. Five years before any of his competitors, Head introduced high-quality metal skis onto the market, an innovation from which his firm could profit (Christensen et al., 1987, pp. 26–59).

In 1950 this entrepreneur founded the Head Ski Company in Timonium, Maryland. He rightly asked, "Why is the sport experiencing little growth in the United States?" He correctly concluded that this sport was not growing because amateur skiers found it hard to maneuver on wooden skis. Such skis performed poorly and were not durable. Although Head's first metal skis cost $75, compared to $20 for the wooden variety, the new breed of skiers preferred the metal skis because they lasted longer and were easier to move around.

People switched to metal skis simply because they liked them enough to pay the extra money. Head, in effect, discovered an unexpected market. His skis had great appeal to beginners and to slightly better skiers. The metal skis could make almost anyone look good on the slopes because they practically turned themselves. Metal skis soon took over the quality market and became widely accepted as ideal for all levels of skiers.

By 1970, Head became the single largest ski manufacturer in the United States, selling more than 125,000 pairs a year at prices ranging from $115 to $175. At that time fiber-reinforced plastic designs loomed as the only challenge to metal skis. This episode illustrates how research and creativity enabled an entrepreneur to gather the technological information that helped produce a superior product and a highly successful business.

SETTING GOALS

Executives tended to view strategies more as means for solving problems rather than for identifying them. The literature echoes this theme. For example, M. Meyerson and E.C. Banfield (1955, p. 312) define a plan as "a course of action which can be carried into effect, which is expected to attain the ends sought." It should be added that in doing their planning executives often find that they have to redefine goals. In reality executives often receive confusing advice about objectives. We know that in the business world CEOs sometimes are asked to come up with a jumble of objectives, including vision statements, mission statements, strategic intents, shareholder value objectives, and customer focuses (Campbell and Alexander, 1997). For example, at times governments adopt reforms whose objectives can have a significant impact on a society; yet over time the interest that government leaders pay to these objectives all too often tends to wane and sometimes to disappear altogether (Schick, 1990).

Nonetheless, despite the possible attendant difficulties, institutions no doubt will continue to identify objectives. Just one case will suffice to illustrate the task of setting goals in order to recognize problems. A bakery in economic distress could decide to market a new, tasty, and nutritious loaf. It could hope to capture a larger share of the market and improve the firm's financial status. As part of its remedial strategy, the company's president might set up a series of ascending sales quotas tied to cash bonuses. He could reason that by providing incentives to the sales force, together with a more definite idea of what he expected of them, employees more likely would meet corporate objectives.

However, meeting preordained goals is just one way, and not always the best way, to judge the worth of remedial action (Chapter 9 discusses this point in greater depth). Despite improving the quality of its bread or the sales ability of its employees, a company still might fail because it sets prices too high.

OBJECTIVITY VS. BIAS

Before discussing the role that problems play in the world, we would benefit by briefly exploring the familiar subject of objectivity versus bias. Authors habitually caution against the influence of prejudice and extol the virtues of reason. Alexander Cornell (1980, p. 164) looked at bias as simply "a conscious or unconscious attitude of evaluating, interpreting, presenting, or using certain data to a subjective, rigid, advocatory manner." Yet no one ever approached a problem with complete objectivity. In the real world, at some time every person brings to a task some predispositions. Texts usually call for eliminating prejudice, an outcome easier asked for than done. If they try, decisionmakers might be able to keep prejudice to tolerable levels.

Executives often tend to favor information that supports their predilections. They might dismiss evidence that challenges their beliefs or demand that researchers provide a level of proof in which executives can have great confidence (Russo and Schoemaker, 1989, pp. xii, 96–98). During the Cuban missile crisis, examined in Chapter 6, some critics suggested that President John F. Kennedy displayed just such an attitude.

Burdening oneself with prejudicial philosophical baggage makes it more difficult to see the broad realities of a situation. A more immediate disability arises when executives become so heavily committed to erroneous or outdated reasoning, intellectual approaches, or analytical methods that they fail to see distortions.

Conversely, individuals who, in the past, successfully championed particular views naturally tend to interrogate the current information base with this success in mind. The force of past commitments need not be overt but can be subconscious. On the other hand, those facing a problem for the first time, having little or no interest, can view it more objectively.

Some maintain that decisionmakers could see the picture more clearly if they looked to the past. By looking retrospectively, one might see that unsubstantiated opinions, not reason, exerted greater weight. Just as in the case of medicine, one might seek a second opinion that might or might not confirm the accuracy of the first.

The neglect of problem solving, in part, stems from a type of bias. Executives exhort their staffs to apply rigorous logic (which usually means to compare alternate courses of action—the core of problem solving). For the most part they do not suggest setting up priorities among the different segments of the information base in order to determine the importance of the various components of problems. They use few or no criteria, standards, or benchmarks by which to judge the status of situations.

EXPECTATIONS

In Chapter 1, we briefly touched on the subject of expectations (e.g., the "revolution of rising expectations"). Another mention is needed at this point. Whether people remain satisfied with conditions largely depends on their expectations. Experiencing deep disappointments often dashes hope. Faced with little opportunity for advancing their lot, either people become resigned to suffering or they revolt. The higher their expectations, the sharper the pain when aspirations collapse. After World War II, many people began to forecast a future of cheap, safe nuclear energy that would bring on a new technological epoch. Nuclear scientists and research engineers proposed all kinds of imaginative projects (Seaborg and Corliss, 1971). Although nuclear power has played a major role in the energy package of several countries, it has not nearly lived up to the ambitious worldwide goals that many advocates had forecast. Those who favor nuclear power consider the failure to meet earlier expectations as a problem.

JUDGMENT

No one can contest the need for good judgment (Hogart, 1987). No other concept has become more pervasive in the literature of decision-making. A judgment based on reviewing a large number of situations stands a good chance of being correct. Such estimations involve values that, in turn, affect preferences. Good decisionmaking requires that whenever possible executives do not limit their examination of information bases solely on narrow considerations. Executives can easily miss the big picture. They also can make mistakes by diagnosing problems according to symptoms rather than by discovering underlying ailments (Bazerman, 1986, pp. 3–4). Executives should try to go beyond the immediate signs.

Decisionmakers must seek a realistic understanding of pertinent circumstances. For example, industrial leaders responsible for developing commercial aircraft had to learn not only about associated technological specifications but also about aesthetic qualities, financial burdens, and ecological dangers. Of importance, executives must rely on judgments in considering the amount of resources to expend for identifying a problem. The size of resource commitment can affect one's ability to diagnose a problem correctly.

The GE–SNECMA Case

The role of good judgment appears in the following case. In 1971 an American firm and a French firm agreed to collaborate on building an advanced commercial jet engine. General Electric (GE) agreed to cooperate with France's Societé Nationale d'Etudes et de Construction de Moteurs d'Aviation (SNECMA) to develop, manufacture, and market such an aircraft engine, the CFM56 (Baranson, 1978, pp. 23–29). This agreement eventually called on both sides to make a difficult judgment that determined ultimate success or failure.

In early deliberations, GE agreed to provide the main engine controls and the core engine technology; SNECMA would furnish the low-pressure engine system and would assume responsibility for mating and fine-tuning each firm's portion of the prototype. GE officials believed that they could capture about half of a potential $10 billion market. SNECMA anticipated that by undertaking a joint venture with GE it could increase its performance in international markets. A future SNECMA engine would benefit the company if the company gained access to the F-101 core engine. The U.S. government had subsidized developing the core for the B-1 bomber, making it the most advanced engine technology in the United States, perhaps in the world.

Each company recognized a major problem in disclosing to the other partner certain technological knowledge concerning its own portion of the engine. On the grounds of protecting national security, in 1971 the U.S. State Department turned down a detailed license request by GE to export technical data to SNECMA. It specifically rejected the transfer of knowledge concerning the export version of the F-101 core engine. U.S. experts believed that during the linkup and fine-tuning of the prototype SNECMA engineers could acquire knowledge of closely held thermodynamic considerations and management techniques in this new and secret technological field.

GE and SNECMA recognized that they had to make a major effort in order to work their way out of this problem. On both sides of the Atlantic, engineers spent considerable time considering the problem. After much thought, GE agreed to lower some of the engine's vital performance parameters, and French engineers agreed to refrain from attending the initial integration and linkup of components and participating in analyzing and balancing the performance of the two firms in this activity. SNECMA engineers had access only to test data relating to their portion of the engine. By agreeing in the mid-1970s to pool their resources, the two companies started to produce an advanced engine that neither would have built on its own. However, this success came about only because each side exerted much effort and thought in coming up with a sound and practical compromise. Each judged correctly what it could and could not do and still have a viable program.

PARTNERS IN THOUGHT

A few other authors share my belief that scholars and executives for the most part have ignored problem identification (Plunkett and Hale, 1982, p. 16). In their classic studies, Frederick Taylor (1912), Frank Gilbreth, (1908, 1912), Chester Bernard (1968), and others paid scant attention to problem identification. Although they do not totally ignore the subject, Peter Drucker (1954) and Herbert Simon (1957) give it short shrift. Joseph L. Massie (1971, p. 52) notes the importance of recognizing the right problem in order to make a good decision, but he does not delve very deeply into the subject. Howard Timms (1967, pp. 67–68) dedicates 2 pages (out of a total 151) to the subject. Stephen J. Andriole (1983, p. 29) devotes just 1 page explicitly in his entire book to this subject, and Bruce F. Baird (1989, p. 10) looks at problem identification but dwells on his belief that "[d]ecision making is oriented toward problem solving."

William Stevenson (1989, p. 4) devotes one paragraph to problem identification, noting that "by adopting a problem focus, you have the advantage of directing attention to the essence of an analysis: to solve a specific problem." He aptly comments that people often jump toward a solution before they sufficiently understand the problem. His advice is but a broad exhortation. He asks that decisionmakers diagnose a problem carefully before reaching for a solution.

Largely ignoring the subject of targeting problems, Thomas W. Knowles (1989) devotes an entire book about management science to models and quantitative techniques. At the outset of their work, Charles H. Kepner and Benjamin B. Tregoe (1981, pp. 33–56) devote one chapter out of a total of nine to explaining the dynamics of identifying problems. They point out that rational decisionmakers should begin their examinations by guessing what has gone or could go wrong with their performance. These scholars refer to "situation appraisals." Van Gundy limits his discussion of subjects such as problem definition, problem structuring, and problem analysis to only the first six pages of his introductory chapter (1981, pp. 1–6).

Authors often speak in terms of "concerns." A concern is any situation that requires action and for which the executive has full or partial responsibility. It includes current deviations, threats, and opportunities and asks such specific questions as: "Are we meeting standards?" "Which problems within the past six months remain unsolved?" "What evidence do we have that we should have concerns?" "How long might a troublesome situation last?"

John Arnold (1992, pp. 9–24) follows a similar line of reasoning, relating problems to "root causes." Executives seek to discover such causes by what Arnold labeled "root cause analysis." Arnold's idea of a problem in some respects reflects the concept in this volume. Root cause analysis begins with a recognition of a gap between what should be occurring and what (allegedly) is not occurring. He suggests that those who lead organizations have to determine if unwanted circumstances trouble them enough to respond.

In their development of "cultural awareness checklists," Craig Hickman and Michael Silva (1984, pp. 65–69) came close to focusing on identifying problems. These checklists prompt decisionmakers to gain greater cultural awareness of the organizations in which they work. They do this by asking pertinent questions. In their study of the pitfalls in decisionmaking, Russo and Schoemaker (1989, pp. xi–xii) offered a few ideas that also seem akin to mine. They advance the notion that just as coaches use training methods to help athletes develop proper sports techniques and habits, those who govern institutions must devise mechanisms that help them select the right information when things go askew. They do this because they want to escape from making errors.

Perhaps more than others, Russo and Schoemaker do provide unique thinking about identifying problems. They devote all of chapter 2 (out of a total of 10 chapters) in their book *Decision Traps* (1989) to decision framing. They call the mental structures that people use to simplify and organize decisions in a highly complex world "frames." By using a framing approach, executives hopefully can understand a little better the complicated world as depicted in the information base.

For example, Decision Trap 1, which they call "plugging in," identifies an error in which one reaches conclusions before thinking through the issue. Here no connection exists between the existence of a problem and the need to remedy it. In their third decision trap, "lack of frame control," these authors define this trap as failing to describe the problem in more ways than one or being influenced unduly by the frames of others (p. xvii).

Conversely, they base the second decision trap, "frame blindness," on the more common practice of decisionmakers to overlook the best alternative and, hence, set out to solve the wrong problem. However, one should remember that, as used here, alternate courses of action belong to solving problems but not to identifying them. Roger Kaufman (1976) presents a useful but limited examination of the subject.

Dorothy Leeds (1988, p. 9) discusses problem identification in terms of the executive's need to ask smart questions. Leeds aims her questions at soliciting answers related to finding unsatisfactory situations. "Knowing how to ask a smart question can get you almost anything you want, anytime." Decisionmakers could improve their competence if they acquired broader skills, such as conducting interviews. For example, a boss could ask, "What are the key qualities that we should look for in people doing certain jobs?" As a standard rule, those responding should articulate the answer in a clear and unambiguous way (pp. 111–112). Sometimes these answers take the form of a positive statement. At other times, the response might come back in the form of a question or a number of questions: "We cannot determine exactly what qualities we require unless the requesting office sends us a complete job description." To study why the requesting office did not send a job description might surface failures within or between departments.

The Centre for the Study of Organisational Change and Development at the University of Bath in England suggests that executives believe that they have a problem if they have discomfort with what they are doing (Eden, Jones, and Sims, 1983, p. 13). If people are dissatisfied with conditions, a problem exists. At first glance, this point sounds a lot like one of the major messages of this book. Yet the Centre's economists still give most weight to problem solving. Although the Centre's study includes a useful examination of the broader historical and theoretical dimensions of the subject, there is much left to be explored.

No other author has given more thought to identifying problems than Alfred W.W. Schoennauer (1981). He begins his work with the following observation: "Problems can only be solved after they have been identified, but the temptation to proceed against symptoms rather than causes appears as an ever present phenomenon in organizations" (p. vii). He devotes about half of his book to discussing finding problems. Schoennauer's study comes closest to the approach used in this volume.

Yet Schoennauer does not explore in-depth situations, factors, resources, historical developments, or thought patterns associated with the act of identifying problems. No criticism is meant here. At the outset, Schoennauer states explicitly that he designed his work as a manual, outlining techniques and methods. His book repeatedly provides useful checklists of what those in charge should or should not look at in any particular situation. In this regard, his work is of great use.

One note of caution: It sometimes becomes difficult to separate problem identification from problem solving. For example, Robert Thierauf's book *A Problem Finding Approach to Effective Corporate Planning* (1987) might lead the prospective reader to anticipate that the author devotes most of his pages to problem identification. Although Thierauf gives problem identification more attention than other writers do, by connecting problem finding so closely to corporate planning (essentially a problem-solving activity), most of his work deals chiefly with problem solving. To Thierauf, planning is fundamental to guiding and directing institutions. As is widely known, problem identification naturally constitutes the first, or at least an early, step in problem solving. Like Schoennauer, Thierauf provides a manuallike, explicit, step-by-step approach to his subject. In addition, executives should realize that they do not face an either/or situation. It is not that they should focus exclusively either on problem solving or on problem identification. Rather, this book suggests that executives should give considerably more weight to problem identification than they have in the past.

SUMMARY

This chapter notes that executives need to make use of awareness, cognition, and goal setting in coming to terms with the task of addressing problems. It points out that dealing with problems constitutes a creative act by which thinkers generate new ideas and concepts. The Head Ski Company and GE–SNECMA cases illustrate how creative executives can overcome formidable difficulties. The chapter briefly discusses other authors who shared some of the ideas developed in this volume but largely neglected the subject of problem identification. It posits that even authors who give some consideration to finding problems place much more emphasis on problem solving. More weight should be given to problem identification than has been done in the past.

CHAPTER 3

The Information Base

Information, an integral part of decisionmaking (Stevenson, 1989, p. 286), relates directly to the knowledge that executives gain to get jobs done. That knowledge can affect their actions in a straightforward way (H. Simon, 1957, p. 68). It is obvious that people differ markedly as to how much information they use in identifying problems and in making decisions (Driver, Brousseau, and Hunsaker, 1993, p. 4). Where to find good, relevant information obviously has become a major task of decisionmakers and their staffs (Brownstone and Carruth, 1979). Paul Lazarsfeld has put the matter well, stating that "man is a data-producing animal" (1959, p. 107). Over the years, scholars have noted the need for good information and have examined the requirements associated with searching for it (Scheffler, 1963). According to Charles Margerison (1974, p. 23): "The major strength of a problem diagnostician is his ability to ask key questions about the causes of a problem and to follow this by gathering relevant information." Actually, executives must have access to information in order to ask apt questions.

DYNAMICS OF HIERARCHY

Problem idenitification usually takes place in organizations. We all know that institutions of significant size are organized as hierarchies, arranged by rank. For the most part, various levels of hierarchies search, assemble,

Figure 3.1
Hierarchical Dynamics of Information Inquiry

Column A	Column B	Column C
Least	Echelons	*Most*
Finding Information	CEOs	Decisionmaking
Arranging	Other Executives	Analyzing
Analyzing	Middle Management	Arranging
Decisionmaking	Workforce	Finding Information

and analyze different categories of information. Those few people at the top exert more power and authority than the more numerous at the bottom. One can measure specific traits in terms of how much effort various levels of hierarchies apply in order to manage the information that they need.

Figure 3.1 illustrates the hierarchical nature of most organizations. At the top in Column B appear CEOs and their immediate staffs. In echelons below reside (high and low) middle managers who support these staffs and help direct the operations of the enterprise. Finally, at the bottom of the organization resides the workforce, the large number of employees who gather most of the information.

Column A of Figure 3.1 lists four traits associated with information management in ascending order of echelon involvement, from the most at the bottom to the least at the top. On the other hand, Column C lists these four same traits in descending order, from the least at the bottom to the most at the top. It must be emphasized that these traits do not appear as watertight compartments. In its activities, each echelon displays some of each trait. Their placement is based upon where they expend most of their effort. Thus, while CEOs and their immediate staffs sometimes discover basic data necessary in their work, they pay most of their attention to discerning how to use the data gained by others to help make wiser decisions.

Notice that the CEOs and their immediate staffs themselves find the least amount of information: They use whatever information is made available (chiefly by others) in helping to make decisions. Conversely, workforces rarely make major decisions, but they usually supply most of the data upon which those decisions are made. Middle managers usually perform most of the arranging and analysis of information. These echelons often contain professional analysts (such as operations researchers) who perform cost-effectiveness, option analysis, queuing theory studies, and other quantitative analyses. CEOs share the responsibility of seeing to it that their staffs have the best information from which to develop sound alternative courses of action and/or make recommendations. CEOs make the decisions.

As one might expect, CEOs take the greatest risks, exercise the most responsibility, address the most critical problems, deal with the widest-ranging problems, and earn the most money. CEOs do not usually pay attention to minutiae and sometimes find it hard to digest the amount of information that flows to them. Information should flow in both directions between top and bottom. The workforce has the greatest physical burden and earns the least money. For example, it has the responsibility of gathering information about specific components relevant to manufacturing a complex jet engine. On the other hand, CEOs also must work with other than hardware data. They must examine data showing the size and strength of the engine market and the international financial factors that affect today's air transport industry—whether a specific jet aircraft will prove profitable and whether it will meet environmental standards. They also have to satisfy the concerns of airlines about fuel consumption and noise output of these engines.

TAPPING THE INFORMATION BASE

The starting point for determining if people confront a problem is the interrogation of the information base (Scheffler, 1963), looking for anomalies or illogical constructs (Kaplan, 1964). James March gets to the heart of the matter in stating, "The study of decision making is, in many ways, the study of search and attention" (1994, p. 23), and search is exactly what executives or their staffs do at the outset when they view an information base. Efraim Turban (1988) points out that executives have to tap the information base to help them evaluate performance. Robin Hogarth (1987, p. ix) echoes a similar role for executives, describing them as people who manipulate their knowledge in making choices. It also is only natural that executives assess their own performance or the performance of their organizations by processing available information.

This process can become more elaborate as decisionmakers increasingly request more relevant, accurate, digested, and up-to-date information. For example, today's business leaders confront the problem of operating in an information-linked and globalized business environment (Laszlo and Laszlo, 1997), which affected them little three or four decades ago. This task demands that they adopt a more complex system for tapping the information base.

Throughout much of the early industrial age, CEOs were disappointed with the performance of employees but had no clear understanding of why people did poor work. Frank Gilbreth (1908, 1912) and other investigators changed this situation by developing time and motion studies. Gilbreth's investigations indicated the extent to which workers were able to get things done expeditiously. He gave industrial firms a way to manipulate information that showed in much more meaningful terms how much employees really worked.

At times the intellect of executives proved inadequate to cast light on the dark shadows of an information base. In order to "see," one needs at least minimum perception. Often observers lacked the ability to see all of the information base or even those portions that should interest them. In these cases, it pays to remember the advice of the famous jazz musician Fats Waller: "If you don't know what it is, don't mess with it" (G. Simon, 1981, p. 540). Waller's message is simple. For the most part, there is more profit in waiting until one knows exactly what the information base has to offer before making decisions or taking action.

KINDS OF UNKNOWNS

Decisionmakers obviously tap information systems in order to eliminate (or reduce) unknowns and to gain relevant facts that they might otherwise ignore. Robert Hayes (1983) suggests that by reducing uncertainty, executives can become aware of unwholesome situations that otherwise might go unnoticed (p. 33). Ignorance might keep executives happy until the reality catches up with them. Like researchers in basic science, decisionmakers face knowns (things they know that they know); unknowns (things that they know that they do not know); and unknown unknowns (things they do not know that they do not know).

Thus, at times executives confront the difficult task of recognizing problems that they previously did not know even existed. Society usually educates people to understand things that they know that they know. For example, some time ago, the world's medical researchers agreed that a disease called "cancer" existed and that they did not know enough about it. Unknown unknowns occur because certain problems appear far beyond the vision of humans. For instance, before actually diagnosing AIDS, people were unaware that they had no knowledge that the disease existed. At the time, AIDS constituted an unknown unknown problem.

With today's rapid rate of change, discovering unknown unknowns poses a formidable task. A chaotic information base stands a better chance of hiding unknown unknowns. On the other hand, by finding discernible trends, one stands a better chance of surfacing unknown unknowns. No doubt, those searching the base can do more to bring a problem to light by structuring problems. Putting bits of information together in logical ways can shift a problem from an unknown to a known or from an unknown unknown to an unknown. Succeeding in this task does not necessarily make the executive happy. The knowns or unknowns that the executive unearths may prove thorny and resistant to solution.

MANAGEMENT INFORMATION SYSTEMS

As all modern executives know, organizations use management information systems (MISs) for gathering and dispensing the information needed for making timely decisions (Brightman, 1971). For the most part, knowledge about the MIS abounds. This discussion focuses only on MISs chiefly as they relate to the process of identifying problems.

Because executives process so much information, they employ computers extensively. They use them for storing, retrieving, extracting, and dispensing data. Computers provide technology support for the MIS used by organizations and systematically aid in detecting problems and in gathering relevant information. The MIS contains indicators that show the health of a company, such as profits, cash flow, inventory levels, financial status, market behavior, productivity levels, schedules, and quality control. These indicators may be displayed as text, tables, graphs, or time series.

For the purposes of this discussion, eight ideas chiefly color the relationship between the MIS and problem identification.

First, the MIS affects an executive's ability to perform one of the major functions discussed here—tap information. Storage and retrieval of huge quantities of information, called data bases, would be much more difficult without computers. In fact, an extensive subdiscipline has emerged relating to the ways in which executives use computers. On the whole, the organization, retrieval, and dissemination of recorded information over time have improved dramatically. As a result, the MIS has become a powerful instrument for interrogating storehouses of information.

Second, although computers have greatly improved the way in which executives can do their jobs, they also have made professionals dependent on them. When the computer crashes, executives are often incapable of carrying on.

Third, in identifying problems, decisionmakers not only want to acquire information but increasingly call for more relevant, accurate, and up-to-date information. An episode on the television program *Chicago Hope*, depicting the exciting drama within a high-quality hospital, vividly displayed the problem of relevant information. This episode, shown in the winter of 1998, clearly illustrated the quandary of a decisionmaker—in this case, a physician—when faced with a conflict between what a computer seems to suggest and what her own experience and instinct tell her to do. On the basis of an analysis of cases within its memory bank, the computer indicates that operating on this patient was inadvisable. Yet the physician's personal observation of such ailments over the years prompts

her to operate in this "life or death" situation. Naturally, in such a television drama the physician operates and all goes well, but executives will
always have to ponder the question of the competing relevance of information derived from computers and from personal experience.

Fourth, in using computers for identifying problems, a paradoxical situation has arisen. Although computers have improved the executive's ability to gain large amounts of information, they also have made it harder
to get specific information. Obtaining specific information lies at the heart
of identifying problems. The computer's ability to deliver increasing
amounts of raw information compounds the challenge of pinpointing the
exact data that might prove relevant in a problem-identifying task.

Fifth, as we know, the effectiveness of MISs can vary. They have proved
most successful in providing information for routine, structured, and anticipated knowledge. Executives obviously look for needed data in their
standard, ongoing reports such as, among others, policy statements, plans,
programs, and budgets.

Sixth, the higher up on the organizational hierarchy problems are identified, the wider and greater the knowledge that executives must have in
applying the MIS. They must look at more categories of human activity
to get a complete picture. For example, top decisionmakers at General
Motors must examine not only industrial functions associated with production but also such factors as financial, marketing, and psychological
functions (dealing with individuals as members of staffs and workforces)
and the political function in sorting out the government's intervention into
business practices (e.g., in improving ecological situations).

Seventh, MISs are touted as devices for solving problems (Turban, 1988,
pp. 5–6). This emphasis fits snugly into the tendency of the literature in
the field to examine problems in terms of remedying rather than identifying them. Today, executives, by and large, seem to give this aspect of
MISs the attention that it deserves.

Eighth, researchers examining information bases should try to achieve
at least a rudimentary understanding of the principles of why MISs work,
rather than slavishly copying their details.

MOTIVATION FOR PRODUCING INFORMATION

Organizations produce data either for descriptive or for prescriptive
purposes (Sanders, 1973, p. 18). Those who supply descriptive information
have no responsibility for what happens to it. They only seek to present
knowledge, hopefully as objectively as possible. This knowledge might
help identify problems. The Bureau of Labor Statistics (BLS) is the federal
government's fact-finding agency for disclosing the status of such items as
wages, industrial relations, injuries, prices, and the standard of living. BLS
has no enforcement function, nor does it carry on programs for improving

the lot of workers. It chiefly presents information and nothing more. Some of these data might identify troubles within the American economy. Other government agencies and private groups have the responsibility of consulting BLS figures in coming up with their economic and social programs.

Individuals and organizations also produce data for prescriptive purposes. These data have the mission of influencing decisions. Executives develop information to indicate their need for resources, wage rates, fringe benefits, legislation, or public sympathy. They aim to influence those who allocate funds to look favorably at their proposals. For example, a record company's marketing department might produce information showing that one of its singers experienced major problems in a certain region of the country. The company might advertise more heavily in that area in order to create more interest in the singer or might decide not to market the singer's records in that part of the country.

By design, political lobbies produce prescriptive information in order to induce legislatures to pass bills favorable to the interests of their clients. For example, labor unions and their affiliated organizations produce data indicating the need for government to take action for increasing employment. Conversely, the National Association of Manufacturers issues production and foreign trade data inferring how foreign competitors take unfair advantage of the American market (e.g., by subsidizing exports). In each case, compilers generate prescriptive information because they have a vested interest in what is done about the problems that the information makes evident.

Put another way, the organization that releases prescriptive data has a major stake in the purpose for which it (or others) uses the data. It often seeks to substantiate its own views or convince others of the merits of its proposed programs. In the Mohole case, cited in Chapter 1, AMSOC, the advocate of the project, produced the information that initially convinced the National Science Foundation and then Congress to allocate funds for the programs.

From the data, people select what is relevant to them. The same forces that shaped the perspectives of organizations about things in general also condition their ideas about information in specific instances. Some people make an entire career out of confirming or invalidating information. Sometimes, the task of determining motivation behind some numbers proves relatively easy. At other times, determining motivation takes great effort.

For example, when systems analysts entered the Pentagon in 1960 with Secretary Robert S. McNamara, they put much more emphasis on numbers in examining problems than supervisory defense offices and high-ranking military officers did before the analyst arrived (U.S. Senate, 1961, pp. 3–6). The military focused more on actual experiences that affected them in war itself, chiefly during World War II and the Korean conflict. Relations between McNamara's analysts and the military became strained.

In part, these antagonisms had to do with the weight that analysts gave to numbers versus what the military had witnessed on the battlefield.

In assembling raw data, one inevitably has to make some arbitrary decisions. Producers of data cannot escape the need to make decisions without the benefit of fixed rules. Those who generate statistics know that permanent guidelines do not always exist. Yet in aggregating or separating numbers, the analyst, in effect, may unintentionally be making judgments about those data and their use. The executive should keep this fact in mind. Very often executives have little choice but to accept the data given them. On other occasions, if they have time, they themselves might prefer to rework statistics that they consider unreliable or distorted.

At any rate, executives should always remain aware of the vulnerabilities of prescriptive knowledge. Authorities often experience considerable troubles in supporting the reliability of data decisions. Opponents can challenge the objectivity of data and how data were produced. Above all, if possible, decisionmakers should rely on more than one source in gathering their data.

NATURE OF THE INFORMATION BASE

In order to grasp the essential elements of the information base, one would do well first to sort out its major parts. Many authors describe these parts, and no extended discussion is necessary here. This study restricts itself to brief explanations. It suggests that in an operational sense the information base is composed of the following components: (1) numbers, (2) artifacts, (3) concepts, (4) behavior, and (5) scenarios.

Numbers

In examining the information base, one must note the critical role that numbers play. We can describe the essence of a document by pointing out the obvious: its information often appears in terms of either language, pictures, or numbers. People seem to have a penchant for writing lists, that is, series of names, words, and again especially numbers, set forth in a certain order. It is hard to explain the exact gravity of problems like a failure in supply or technological obsolescence without using numbers. Those who query information bases naturally prefer that numbers appear in an unambiguous way. However, as pointed out in Chapter 1 (Figure 1.1), executives often confront unclear numbers. It is not enough to report that today's production ran "fairly high." People who need information prefer to know that the factory produced 100 black, six-cylinder Ford Mustang convertibles per day. This information can give a CEO the specific information that he or she needs.

Nor can numbers always picture situations correctly. How do you describe the morale of workers on the factory's production lines by using numbers? How do numbers tell a CEO how the workers feel about a certain foreman? Taking a poll represents one way, but executives rarely, if ever, take formal polls.

Yet numbers remain one of the most effective ways of getting to the heart of certain kinds of problems. To judge their performance, modern executives use the numbers contained in performance ratings, despite the fact that some employees might believe that such numbers are unfair. In addition, no other reasonable way exists of expressing the dimensions of a company's debt, profitability, and cash flow. How could the costs and effectiveness of competing technological projects be compared without, in some way, explaining their chief characteristics in numbers? After all, one commercial transport aircraft can fly just so many miles with certain cargo loads at designated rates of speed before increasing fuel and other costs tell airline executives that returns are diminishing.

Furthermore, in addressing raw data, one inevitably has to learn to appreciate that at times numbers themselves become important issues. The U.S. Bureau of Labor Statistics can pose a problem for politicians by reporting a high unemployment figure of 15 percent. A high percentage of people out of work could turn voters away from incumbents. American politicians use unemployment figures as key arguments in political campaigns.

Economics today has become a social science very dependent on numbers. Economists educated in the first part of the twentieth century thought about economic phenomena in the form of concepts such as supply and demand, market-determined wages, and the market as a self-correcting mechanism. For the most part, they used qualitative terms in addressing the problems of their day.

Conversely, modern economists learn their discipline by becoming expert in some quantitative expressions. Formulas dot their intellectual landscapes. Numbers come close to determining almost all (and some argue all) aspects of their discipline. In fact, modern economists call their discipline "econometrics," showing its tight connection with measurement. Today's economist often lives and dies by the numbers.

Modern executives use numbers and sometimes rigorous quantitative analysis in targeting undesirable situations. If they cannot apply quantitative methods themselves, they hire analysts to do it. The degree to which they can employ quantitative techniques effectively varies according to the type of problem that they are investigating. Usually, the greater the technical content of a problem, the more the need for rigorous quantitative calculations.

Artifacts

Artifacts are objects made by human workers. Today, for the most part, they refer to the physical elements that make up the technological (hardware) aspects of a society and, of interest here, of information bases. In searching for the past, archeologists look for such physical items as urns, pots, dwellings, temples, burial sites, weapons, and farming and household implements. In large part, today's observers seem to emphasize the artifacts of computers, software, copiers, and office technologies in discussing modern information and communications systems.

As is widely known, today the artifacts of computers, including management information systems and communications equipment, are improving at a fairly rapid rate (Walsh, 1981). The early computers could do little more than "crunch numbers." Today, they can perform computations on relevant information having a bearing on decisions and can conduct "what-if" analysis. They are just beginning to interact with the intellectual steps that executives take in making decisions (Turban, 1988, p. 14). Can modern computers think? Some claim that artificial intelligence is here or is on its way.

Likewise, during the past decades, communications equipment has improved greatly. The transistor and the microchip replaced the vacuum tube, leading to much smaller communications devices requiring much less power. Microwave links now crisscross the country. The space program gave us artificial satellite relays, and by including traveling wave tubes, these satellites enjoyed television capabilities (Finn, 1967, pp. 293–309). Engineers connected computers to these improved communications systems, allowing them to talk to each other. Other advances in these artifacts abound, but the foregoing discussion suffices for the purposes of this study.

Concepts

An information base contains more than artifacts. It also consists of generalized ideas and abstract notions. In short, executives apply concepts in sorting out specific experiences and translating them into general rules or principles. In formulating concepts, decisionmakers provide a means for dividing a body of knowledge into logical separate components. Looked at another way, the human mind tends to absorb from the information base concepts that help it accommodate the generalities (concepts) and specifics contained in that base.

In formulating concepts, one converts specific experiences into general rules or classes. In order to develop concepts, executives first must identify key traits and then determine how these characteristics are logically connected. This process resembles the method used in identifying problems. Concepts also may serve as norms or models that tell executives when situations or conditions in the information base fluctuate or stand still. Executives often make their decisions in responding to which event occurs. For example, CEOs increasingly have adopted the concept that in addition to earning a profit, commercial firms should follow a policy of contributing to the welfare of the society in which they exist (Bowen, 1969, pp. 72–74). In the nineteenth century, rarely did a CEO hold such a concept.

Behavior

In tapping their information sources, executives naturally have to consider the behavior that individuals and groups exhibit (Hull, 1943). In its most general sense, "behavior" denotes how people conduct themselves. Behavior obviously affects all that executives do. Inasmuch as decision-makers usually call on a wide range of organizations to conduct today's business, the institutional dimensions of the information base have become very complex. Organizations continually have to consider such questions as: "How much delegation of authority would benefit a company?" Subordinates complain about overly centralized and dictatorial rule. "Where do centers of responsibility lie within the organization?" Most often, organizations set down general ideas about how people rearrange organizations to contend with changes in problems. For example, after World War II, the United States established the Atomic Energy Commission (AEC) to take advantage of the opportunities, and address the problems, that the new nuclear technology brought to the fore.

As the price of oil soared and the United States faced a momentous problem in its oil supply, the nation switched to an executive type of organization—the Department of Energy—with its more direct lines of authority than the AEC (with its committee type of organization) exhibited. With an executive department in charge, government leaders believed that technicians could tap information on energy in general (including nuclear) in a more effective way.

Scenarios

Scenarios depict settings (models) in which decisionmaking takes place. They help executives to cope with and hopefully overcome the uncertainty that so often plagues institutions (Georgantzas and Acar, 1995). In essence, a scenario is a narrative in which the dynamics of participants can lead to one or more decisions or outcomes. Institutions employ scenarios so that their members can participate in decisionmaking situations for educational purposes. In the process, participants interact with each other (Turban, 1988). Scenarios illustrate how executives think and act in specific situations. Executives can fashion scenarios from the facts that they derive from the information base.

By employing scenarios, an organization's leaders hope to gain insights into the actions people take in real situations. As a result, players do not have to experience actual privations for making a mistake, as would happen in real life. Players in scenarios know that to some degree realism is lacking. Nonetheless, these players can discover the problems associated with a particular undertaking. Scenarios also can teach executives valuable lessons. For decisionmakers, scenarios represent a proven vehicle for helping people come to grips with certain kinds of problems.

Organizations sometimes use technologies employing scenarios. For example, simulators employ scenarios. Simulators can help train people to use technologies. Both commercial and military aviators have long used the Link Trainer (an airplane cockpit that simulates actual flight) in pilot training. Airlines and air forces increasingly have come to depend on simulators. The U.S. Air Force found that it could use a variety of simulators to instruct in many facets of flying without actually putting pilots in real aircraft that consume a great deal of expensive fuel. Some scenarios describe the dynamics of responding to uncontrollable factors by applying damage-limiting devices. Both civilian and military aviation have benefited as their executives have resorted to simulators and scenarios to train future pilots and other aviation personnel without incurring high costs. Enterprises other than aviation (e.g., communications and sports) have gained by employing simulators.

INFORMATION TECHNOLOGIES

One cannot discuss the problem identification aspects of management information systems without mentioning, at least briefly, the rapid pace at which new hardware has emerged. Researchers have produced new technologies so fast that we rightly can call their development a revolution. Observers suggest that the impact of this revolution dwarfs those that came before. Although many technologies helped produce current information systems, eight stand out: (1) advanced semiconductors; (2) advanced computers; (3) fiber optics; (4) cellular technology; (5) satellite technology; (6) advanced networking; (7) improved human-computer interaction; and (8) digital transmission (Albert, Papp, and Kemp, 1997, pp. 84–85). Notice that computers and ancillary equipment are only two of the many technologies that brought about these rapid developments. This point merits consideration because all too often it seems that observers think and write as if computers alone accounted for the information revolution.

It comes as no surprise that this revolution improved the capabilities of executives to identify problems. Sometimes executives can ferret out a problem contained within an information base only by assessing huge amounts of data. To do this without the new technologies would take an exceedingly long time at an excessive cost. At times, only by applying these technologies can executives convert chaos to ordered information, the starting point for seeking identification. As we come to the end of the twentieth century, we are not sure if that revolution has begun to wane or whether we will experience continued rapid growth in these technologies in the years to come.

SUMMARY

This chapter examines the collection of facts, events, concepts, and behavior called the information base. In order to identify problems, decisionmakers naturally must gain access to this base. The greater the skills that individuals display in tapping this body of knowledge, the more they will succeed in carrying out their decisionmaking tasks. It is clear that all problem identification must begin with the step of gaining access to the information base. The motivation for developing data can differ among people and organizations. Descriptive data tend to be more objective, and people and organizations other than those that produced that data exploit them to support their own policies and programs. Prescriptive information tilts toward the ideas and programs of the agency developing the data. For the sake of analysis, information bases can be broken down into the following components: numbers, artifacts, concepts, behavior, and scenarios. The technology of information has experienced revolutionary growth in recent decades, and this new hardware, including simulators, is of great help to the executive who would identify problems.

CHAPTER 4

Information Tendencies

People responsible for tapping into available information bases obviously should understand the various characteristics of their components. The more executives know about these traits, the more effectively they can use information.

If decisionmakers must learn to identify problems effectively before they try to solve them, they have to become aware of the shifts and changes that information experiences over time. To do this, they must gain considerable knowledge about the nature and dynamics of information itself. They have to determine if the information contains worthwhile messages and what those messages might be. They have to produce reports collected from a variety of sources, carefully collated and analyzed by experts (Kegley and Wittkopf, 1987, p. 118).

PATTERNS

In doing their jobs, executives prefer that data found in information bases appear in the form of patterns. We indicated earlier, however, that all too often this information appears in a chaotic state. Consequently, as much as possible, analysts must learn to look for and hopefully find logic amid the confusion.

A pattern displays this logic. It is an arrangement in which components generally share common characteristics. Effective decisionmakers have the ability to differentiate idiosyncratic elements of the information base from logical ones. Information containing peculiarities may not contain a usable message, or executives may find it difficult to decipher the eccentricities. From time to time, decisionmakers might extract serviceable ideas from a disordered universe, but to do this requires considerable ingenuity and great effort.

If patterns show events starting to move in new directions, executives should become alert to the possibility of new problems. Deviations from regular, predictable, and unvarying patterns could indicate types of unsatisfactory situations. By recognizing and understanding patterns, analysts can have greater confidence in their ability to discover unwanted circumstances. Of course, such deviations might also indicate opportunities.

Of great importance, because patterns follow logic, executives can use them for forecasting. By forecasting, executives have an opportunity to discover problems coming up in the future. Effective bosses respond swiftly when they become aware of patterns that illustrate new adverse directions. Yet we should remember that executives can best recognize patterns if they remain detached. As Heifetz and Laurie aptly note, "Business leaders have to be able to view patterns as if they were on a balcony. It does them no good to be swept up in the field of action" (1997, p. 125).

TRENDS

For the most part those searching for problems look for trends in the information bases, the prevailing direction of the products, organizations, and events under investigation. Wolfgang Schmitt, the CEO of Rubbermaid, made this point quite explicitly by observing, "We operate on the premise that our job is to identify trends" (Walden and Lawler, 1993, p. 2). Trends relate closely to patterns. In fact, people tend to use the two words interchangeably. In technical terms, the word *trend* stands for a data flow that persists over time (e.g., up or down, faster or slower). We can see physical "trends" in topography. The elevation of a valley can rise incrementally until the land becomes the foothills of a mountain range.

Rising or falling numbers can tell decisionmakers whether their enterprises are prospering or failing, and to what extent. Numbers showing an upward movement in profits or cash flow convey the welcome message that one's business is prospering. Of importance to manufacturing engineers, numbers can tell if the scheduling of production lines will enable them to meet milestone obligations. Conversely, an upward trend in costs and absenteeism tells a different story. It might indicate that a manufacturing industry increasingly lives in peril of losing its competitive edge. Rising costs could make profitability difficult or impossible. A lengthy downward slope in financial resources could mean the firm might face bankruptcy. Conversely, a declining debt slope might signal a financially strengthened company.

Investigations specifically serve the mission of "identifying trends." Companies normally view this function as marketing (finding out what customers want). Whatever prism executives use, in looking for trends, they are interested in change. By definition, most of the time trends reflect change.

Most of the trends that executives acquire come in the form of estimates (Russo and Schoemaker, 1989, pp. 80–81). Those responsible for gathering and interrogating estimates live with judgments that roughly fix such traits as worth, size, weight, and amount. Unless executives have accurate estimates, they stand little chance of dealing with unsatisfactory conditions. In the commercial world, operators frequently look to program and budget statements to discover what institutions accept as true representations of facts.

It is well known that most decisionmakers are familiar with the foregoing aspects of trends. They also know much less about the following three phenomena associated with trends—discontinuities, paradigms, and quantum jumps.

Discontinuities

Some perceptive observers noted that "[d]iscontinuous change requires a break with the past, perhaps even the deliberate destruction of certain elements of the current system (Nadler et al., 1995, p. 37). A discontinuity, then, is a sudden, sharp rupture or gap in an ongoing pattern; it takes the form of an acute turn in direction. A firm facing a discontinuity might see rough times ahead or, conversely, unexpected and unprecedented success. In either case, the firm experiences a discontinuity rather than merely an incremental step. If a small retail firm lacks a sound financial basis, disappointing Christmas sales could force it out of business. Conversely, if Christmas sales rise sharply, enterpreneurs might make up for past slow sales, produce profits, and pay dividends to stockholders.

Paradigms

A paradigm is a sharp discontinuity in a trend that introduces a novel set of enduring conditions. Robert Merton (1957), an American philosopher of science, suggested the use of paradigms in studying the relationship between science and society. To Merton, a paradigm was a systematic statement of the basic assumptions, concepts, and propositions employed by a school of analysts at and for any given time.

To Thomas Kuhn (1962, pp. 43–51), a paradigm is a prevailing theoretical system. At any given time, he suggests, scientists share a set of beliefs about their "normal" world, which constitutes the dominant paradigm. They remain content to limit their explorations within its boundaries. At certain times, some adventurous investigators make new discoveries beyond existing borders. A paradigm shift takes place, illuminating characteristics different from those that came before. Knowledge increasingly becomes obsolete, and another generation of scientists arises to exploit new frontiers suggested by the characteristics of the newly found paradigm.

For example, when Isaac Newton formulated the fundamental laws of mechanics, leading to the formulation of the law of gravity, he laid down a new paradigm. For many years, physicists worked hard to refine, elaborate on, and criticize the core of Newtonian physics. In the twentieth century, Albert Einstein's new physics reached beyond the boundaries of Newton's world by establishing a new paradigm. A new generation of scientists arose and worked hard to discover anomalies that subsequently led scientists to fashion a yet newer paradigm. In effect, Einstein's seminal work had ushered in a novel paradigm.

Executives likewise work within existing paradigms, formed by the knowledge contained within their information base. Most researchers spend their time finding extant information. At the same time, a few pioneering investigators seek to discover anomalies within this information paradigm. Sometimes these few are entrepreneurs, people who assume the risk and direction of new business ventures. By attempting the difficult and the untried, entrepreneurs produce new paradigms. Once executives surface a new body of information, they can work to bring heretofore unknown knowledge to the front. For example, before the "scientific management" contributions of Frederick Taylor (1912) and Frank Gilbreth (1908), management's paradigm of the workplace depended on intuitive and, for the most part, qualitative methods. Steven Jobs and Steven Wozniak, the originators of the pioneering Apple personal computer firm, were entrepreneurs who moved beyond the bounds of existing technology and ushered in a new industry paradigm.

Discussing paradigms has relevance in addressing problem identification. At any given time, the information base available to decisionmakers constitutes a limited paradigm. To the degree possible, leaders in organizations attempt to exploit all the information that they can within existing boundaries. On occasion, researchers unearth important facts that do not fit with the extant information paradigm. They then seek to uncover another paradigm that yields new and useful insights. Of course, the new paradigm also triggers new problems. Certainly, as industrialists increasingly came to use time-motion studies, they achieved a new paradigm involving more effective management of human resources. This new set of conditions contained some additional and different problems. In addition to other important factors, by the early and middle twentieth century this new paradigm assisted American entrepeneurs in building a large number of very potent industrial enterprises.

Quantum Jumps

A quantum jump is an abrupt transition in a trend from one set of parameters to another. A discontinuity always begins a quantum jump. For example, it occurs when a new technology's performance exceeds that of an older one by a significant factor (Sanders, 1987). A sharp break exists between the speed of piston engine aircraft and jet engine aircraft. Jet aircraft fly so much faster than propeller-driven aircraft that we measure the speed of advanced jets in terms of sound (mach) rather than in traditional terms of miles per hour.

As a result of this jump, a qualitative change takes place. The shift appears so great that one no longer deals with mere additional increments of improvement but with appreciably altered circumstances. In other words, the quantum jump ushers in a new age that changes entire environments.

For instance, the advent of the commercial jet transport aircraft not only affected flight times but also drastically changed how airlines did business. Transatlantic airliners could fly from the East or West Coasts of the United States to Europe without stopping en route. The way the airlines scheduled flights, serviced passengers, procured aircraft, operated at airports, advertised, managed their finanaces, and other activities all changed in a major way. The Concorde also brought about dynamic alterations. An executive in New York could board this airliner in the morning and attend a meeting in London on the same day (although high costs prevented the Concorde from servicing the mass aviation market). One merely has to observe how the aviation industry conducted its business after the arrival of jets to see a quantum jump.

DOCUMENTS

To a large degree, executives find information in a great variety of documents. Of course, among other uses, documents assist executives in making decisions. Stephen Andriole makes the important point that "[p]roblem solutions which are poorly documented generally go unappreciated and unwanted" (1983, p. 147). Thus, reports and memoranda often become the life blood in an organization's communications systems.

One special problem has appeared in today's reports that challenges the effectiveness of decisionmakers. Top executives have become concerned with the abysmally poor writing that they often find in these documents. Decisionmakers understand neither the definition nor the solution of problems if they appear in writing that one finds difficult to comprehend. Because of the increased scientific and technological nature of modern problems, it is crucial that technical writers communicate in clear and understandable language. The general problems of communicating through documents have built up a huge literature and need no elaboration here.

Of importance to this discussion, documents provide information that tells executives if unsatisfactory situations exist. It pays to examine briefly some of the key documents that executives prepare and consult in their efforts to discover problems. A document type is classified by the kind of information that it contains. Among the better-known types of documents that executives use today are those that deal with planning, programming, and/or budgeting (Sanders, 1973, pp. 42–43). Planning, programming, and budgeting documents have a direct bearing on the allocation of resources, a key activity that largely determines the success or failure of executives in directing their organizations.

POLICIES AND PLANS

At one time or another, every student of decisionmaking has sought the meaning and uses of policies and plans. *Policies* refer to courses of action designated to overcome problems by meeting organizational goals and values. We generally regard *planning* as a method of suggesting ways to achieve goals. Some practitioners hold that planning serves as an organizational device, citing where an organization wants to go in the long term; however, Peter Drucker (1974, p. 122) suggests that planning relates to the question, "What *should* our business be?" In answering this question, executives have to understand the problems that entrepreneurs faced when starting the business in the first place.

Drucker's point should be examined before addressing questions like "What is our business?" and "What will our business be?" Plans usually contain relatively long-range objectives. For the most part, plans indicate where executives want to go and in general how they expect to get there. Plans usually do not cite the particulars of needed resources.

PROGRAMS

On the other hand, programs cite the details, especially those relating to needed resources. Often, program documents are said to express corporate strategies because they contain the resources that firms or public agencies develop to make their ambitions come to life (Collis and Montgomery, 1998, pp. 71–83). Therefore, programming documents, more often than other statements, reveal the information that higher-level executives need for identifying problems. For example, programming documents present the evidence that backers of new activities can cite for remedying situations with which they are dissatisfied. Programming relates to conducting the operations of an institution: The program will lay out x money for personnel recruitment, y money for research and development, and z money for manufacturing.

Programming also has become important in unexpected areas. For instance, programming has become increasingly of value in educational activities and in the insurance business; professionals have placed increased emphasis on presenting new and imaginative programming ideas for social functions, business sessions, and workshops. Programs specify resources and the missions for which executives earmark them. Decisionmakers in public agencies as well as CEOs (and their staffs) in private firms determine resource commitments. They have to determine if they are placing these resources in the right places. This task becomes critical if CEOs want to direct the efforts of their organizations toward uncovering the most significant problems.

Programs usually come about as the result of a competition among rival groups in an organization or among organizations. These competitors expend much energy convincing leaders of the logic and opportunities of their proposals in terms of the number and types of resources. Requests appear as line items, usually in the amounts that organizations conclude they need to perform their missions. In short, decisionmakers try to gain knowledge about the resources that they require and within a resource allocation system. Again, as a first step, institutions have to identify problems.

Widespread Use

There is no consensus about the degree to which decisionmakers have adopted programming. Certainly, many businesses have not adopted programs. Although its use by federal agencies receives the most attention, private companies increasingly have come to use programs. As a rule, large corporations, especially those dependent on advancing technology, have recruited programming experts. Top leaders in private industry as well as in government, in one way or another, have resorted to some type of programming, in part to provide a means of identifying problems.

In the 1960s, local governments (e.g., Dayton, Ohio) adopted programming to assist them with resource problems and decisions. St. Louis, a city with a long history of budget reforms, changed its budgeting dramatically in 1975 and in 1989 printed its first program and performance budget. As a result, the mayor and his line departments came to do business in program terms, especially making resource trade-offs (Rubin and Stein, 1990).

At the end of the 1980s, Bromon Aircraft, a Puerto Rican private firm, had approached the final design stage of the BR-2000, a medium-lift transport plane, and had made plans for a first flight. In addition to an accounting package (a small computer system called MAX), Bromon bought a program package and used it in developing the aircraft (Garfein, 1988). Inasmuch as successful automotive operations have to consider quality, price, performance, and a fast-to-market strategy, executives in the industry have turned to a program management support system that combines procedures, tools, and experienced people. This combination seems to provide a total approach to directing automobile programs (Urbaniak, 1991).

Budgets

Budgets convert the arrangement of information as found in programs in ways consistent with an organization's style of doing business. Sometimes budgets perform the same function as programs (used for resource allocation). In larger establishments, budgets differ from programs in that very often they meet the demands of outside authorities. In the private sector, budgets inform boards of directors, stockholders, the public, or the government of the company's status. We all know that in the American federal system the executive branch develops the budget. The president transmits the federal budget to Congress, which may or may not appropriate funds. Obviously, programs are rearranged to conform to legislation passed by Congress.

Integration

Executives often tend to combine components into a whole, and this predilection has its implications for the documents that they use. They seek to establish and maintain what they believe are more direct and consistently logical connections among these documents. For this reason they do not always clearly separate planning, programming, and budgeting. They use such labels as "planning, programming, and budgeting," "program budgeting," "program management," "program plans," and "strategic planning and programming" (Sanders, 1973, pp. 19, 38, 42–43). In administering their institutions, executives usually give most attention to the programming function. It is within the programming documents that they usually find their major problems and allocate resources to solve them. Once staffs and other subordinates understand the importance of these documents, they tend to abide by them.

Special Studies

In addition, from time to time, both private companies and public agencies conduct special studies that point out especially troublesome problems. In querying programs, executives discover what has gone wrong and in which ways. Although special investigations query programs for a number of reasons, identifying problems constitutes the chief mission. Here analysts look for abnormalities and errors associated with resource allocations. Thus, more often than not, programs contain fundamental questions concerning the use of resources. Executives use these data to determine if their organizations are performing in unacceptable, adequate, or superior ways.

To make this determination, decisionmakers ask such questions as: "Are the owners of the enterprise dissatisfied with the results of a particular program?" "Do executives make effective use of the information that their subordinates collect and analyze?" "When do bosses have to make their results available?" "What specific resources do they lack?" Such questions often form the basis for special studies that look into program data more deeply or differently than executives usually do.

Comparing Programs

How well decisionmakers conduct comparisons depends on their general knowledge and their investigatory prowess. More than anything else, the quality of their questioning is influenced by the kinds of queries, the availability of data, and the relationship between the two. It is well to reiterate here that more than other documents, program documents are designed to provide organizations with the information that they need to identify pertinent concrete problems. Programmers examine conditions, develop new information, interpret program results, and check the completeness of programs. What's more, they do this on a periodic basis.

The degree to which executives have an effective problem identification capability depends in large part on how well their staffs analyze programs. These staffs must be able to compare the similarities and differences associated with the contents of programs. Analysts have to examine these data from a baseline that reaches from past to current activities and sometimes into the future. They have to examine such items as resource input, resource output, operational procedures, or some combination of these. For instance, some critics of the federal government have charged that public officials stress resource inputs because it is easier to do that than to examine outputs. Moreover, executives also profit by comparing variations among projects within a single program.

Comparing programs in order to detect problems offers an attractive approach for several reasons. First, this comparison can provide information on the importance of alternate problems contained within the information base, and it can do this in comparable terms. Second, it can help reduce the need for organizations to rely on elusive "control of experiment" methods. This result eases and makes less complicated the task of targeting problems. Third, it offers an opportunity to identify exceptional performance and to study the differences among projects undergoing analysis.

Decisionmakers can come up with a sound appraisal of programs by determining which consequences result from these programs or which result from other influences (Rutman, 1977). Success in such endeavors largely depends on how many investigators are available, their competence, and how well they know the specific problems under examination.

In recent years as social attitudes change, so too have the kinds and types of information that decisionmakers have to consider. Today, executives in the private sector frequently have to appraise their programs in relation to more than profits. At times they have to answer to complaints about pollution or unethical conduct. Firms now have to take into account social costs, and these could appear in the program. The following example illustrates this point.

Since the early days of research, many biological investigators have given little thought to the ethics of conducting experiments on animals. Today, animal rights groups have forced these laboratories to think more carefully about their experiments in terms of cruelty. Do animals have rights? Have laboratories violated these rights? Any effort to improve the treatment of animals has its impact on whether researchers can gain the knowledge that they seek. Does society demand that it should forego certain cures if they can be developed only by inflicting pain on animals? These laboratories might well incur additional costs in improving the treatment of experimental animals, and these costs, no doubt, will be reflected in the laboratory's programs.

Executives often use budgets to discover problems, especially if they do not have access to programs. Of course, budgets are particularly useful when investigators look for financial troubles.

DATA DEVELOPMENT

In identifying problems, executives benefit if they have thought beforehand about the specific questions that they ask and how these relate to the analytical methods that they use. They often find that the task of selecting and collecting data may prove the least attractive aspect of any appraisal. At times this effort becomes quite routine and boring. However, assembling data ranks among the most important steps made in constructing the information base. Major sources of these data are (1) interviews, (2) mailed questionnaires, (3) onsite observations, (4) peer group ratings, (5) standardized written texts, (6) project and other program records, (7) federal and state government statistics (e.g., from the Census Bureau or the Bureau of Labor Statistics), (8) performance tests or other physical evidence, (9) clinical observations, (10) financial, cost accounting, and operations research results, and (11) documents such as minutes, progress reports, and public releases.

Analysts find it useful to consult several sources for their data. If they find that sources tend to agree as to the accuracy and meaning of their data, they can have greater confidence that the conclusions they have reached are valid. Whenever possible, those making appraisals should provide systematic information about the results of programs and the degree of confidence that they attached to these results.

SUMMARY

Decisionmakers must understand that no matter how random information might seem, they have to seek some order. The various forms of information arrangements—the patterns, trends, discontinuities, quantum jumps, and paradigms—discussed in this chapter provide different understandings. Although these characteristics present a broad framework for analysis, sooner or later executives must consult the information that appears in the documents they use. These practical documents, among others, relate to the plans, budgets, and especially programs that have become common in both private and public institutions. More than other documents, program documents contain the amount, type, and detail of information that assist the executive most often.

CHAPTER 5

Different Prisms

This chapter explores the different ways in which decisionmakers look at the information base and the unwanted circumstances that it sometimes contains. This chapter asks, From whose perspective is the problem being viewed?

FROM WHOSE PERSPECTIVE?

Like beauty, the existence, immediacy, and severity of a problem lie in the eye of the beholder. Donald Gause and Gerald Weinberg (1982, p. 8) observe that to take hold of a problem one has to ascertain at the outset, "Whose problem is it?" This task deserves major attention early in any investigation. Not everyone is concerned about gaps existing between what is and what ought to be. At any given time, individuals and groups react to existing conditions differently.

In other words, how one describes and appreciates a problem varies from observer to observer and from time to time. Researchers at the University of Bath understood this diversity well and suggested, "Problems, then, are very individual things in the sense that different persons might see quite different problems in the same situations" (Eden, Jones, and Sims, 1983, p. 15).

The Tanaca Story

It is well to begin examining the phenomenon of peering at problems from different viewpoints in human terms. The saga of a village in Mexico points out how "whose perspective" affects societies still mired in subsistence living (Sanders, 1957). This case illustrates how views about problems differ among peoples who are about to receive a major technological innovation, in this case, electric power. In the late 1950s, Mexico conducted an ambitious program to electrify the entire country, bringing this convenience to many hamlets. Not all these rural communities examined their problems in the same way or as carefully as others to see how they could best take advantage of this technological boon.

Tanaca is a small Tarascan Indian village, tucked away in the Sierra Madre Occidental of Mexico. Located about 10 miles from the main road, it was inaccessible by vehicle during much of the rainy season. Tanacans survived on subsistence farming, but the town did have a small-scale lumber enterprise. It operated a primitive sawmill, powered by a truck engine. With the government about to connect the village to electric lines, leaders in Tanaca examined their problems closely to discern how this new technology might help them.

For instance, the men of the village were building a basketball court for night games, which at first glance might seem odd. One might conclude that the Tanacans had misread the problems they faced. To improve their tender economy, should they not first have built an infrastructure designed to make the most effective use of electric-powered tools? Yet they knew exactly what they had to do. The young farmers of the village lived a monotonous existence, enjoying few diversions and pleasures. Every day they awoke, ate some tortillas for breakfast, went out to tend the fields, returned home at sunset, ate supper and/or frequented the cantinas, and finally went to bed.

The village elders aimed to entice the youth away from the cantinas where the men went nightly to get drunk. They preferred that these young men spend their evenings playing some wholesome sport. They wanted to remedy a serious problem among young Mexican men—alcoholism.

Why did the villagers in Tanaca carefully examine their community to identify the problems that electric power might help remedy, whereas other rural communities did not? Tanacans displayed what the Spanish call *empuje*, which is the energy, drive, or motivation of people to better themselves. Years before electricity was anticipated, the people of Tanaca had constructed a clay pipeline from a source of pure water miles away in the nearby mountains to the village square. However, when electric power came, other villages, some astride the main highway, did little more than tap illegally into the distribution lines to light their houses.

The Tanacans saw their problems differently than villagers living nearer the main highway. With transportation accessible the latter confronted easier tasks and had more opportunities for advancement. Although the people of Tanaca had a more difficult task, they had greater incentive. Because they had identified problems, they were better able to solve them. Inasmuch as they had thought through their problems carefully before-hand, they could exploit the new technology when it arrived to their best advantage. The village elders captured the admiration of the youth because these more mature leaders had thought in long-range social terms.

The Osirak Raid

Some episodes clearly display that over time people can change their minds about perspectives. The following case illustrates a change at the highest national decisionmaking levels. On June 7, 1981, Israeli warplanes destroyed Iraq's Osirak nuclear reactor ("Israeli Warplanes," pp. 385–386). Prime Minister Menachem Begin charged that Iraq was developing this facility to produce atomic bombs whose eventual target would be Israel. The Israelis argued that Iraq's nuclear program posed a major threat to the survival of the Jewish state (Feldman, 1981).

The United States immediately condemned the Israeli attack, and 12 days later the U.S. ambassador to the United Nations, Jeanne Kirkpatrick, cast a vote in the world organization censuring Israel for the raid. She likened the Israeli attack to the brutal Soviet invasion of Afghanistan ("U.N. Condemns Israel," pp. 434–435). By a unanimous vote, the Security Council declared the attack a gross violation of the United Nations Charter and the norms of international conduct. Most of the world seemed to believe that Iraq's nuclear enterprise posed no problem critical enough to warrant Israel's military action.

One can assume with confidence that a decade later the United States probably changed its perspective about the 1981 Israeli action. During the Gulf War of 1991 the armed forces of the United States and its coalition partners threw the Iraqis out of Kuwait, which the Iraqis had invaded some months earlier. At the time the United States did not mention explicitly the impact that the Israeli raid on Osirak might have exerted on that war.

If, during the Gulf War, U.S. leaders had thought about the 1981 raid at all, most likely they would view it through another prism. One cannot conclude positively that if Israel had not destroyed the Osirak facility, coalition forces would have faced Iraqi atomic arms. Yet between 1981 and 1991, had the Osirak raid not taken place, Iraq might have built a nuclear arsenal. Without doubt, a nuclear-armed Iraq would have been a much more dangerous enemy. The United States could not have assumed that Saddam Hussein would not have launched a nuclear attack. Although the United States and the United Nations did not consider Iraq's atomic activities as a major threat in 1981, 10 years later they must have given quiet thanks that Israel had foreclosed that option for the Iraqis.

ASSUMPTIONS VS. THE KNOWN

In changing prisms from which to view the world, obviously one must separate facts from beliefs and symptoms. The ability or the inability to make this distinction helps determine probable outcomes. In order to gain proper insight into a specific problem, one should (1) place boundaries around cores of similar information, (2) apply criteria for comparing different parts of a total problem, and (3) develop or choose yardsticks that executives might employ in judging the dimensions of the total problem and its components.

INCREASED DEMAND FOR KNOWLEDGE

Successful officials often have to develop a knack for dealing with the information base under varying levels of stress. At times, however, a person may not have enough strength and knowledge to locate and define a major problem. A U.S. Air Force story brings this point home. At the height of the cold war, a general was berating a junior officer for failing to prevent a major problem from developing. The junior officer could contain himself no longer and finally blurted out, "Sir, I could do nothing to have prevented this messy situation." (All the information that he possessed had proved inadequate to handle events.) The general reportedly answered: "I know that, but there are two kinds of officers that I cannot stand: incompetent ones and unlucky ones, and I do not have the time to determine which are which in any specific case."

In many situations, executives cannot offer a plausible excuse for failing to identify the right information; in others, such an explanation might satisfy superiors. Yet there is such a thing as too much information. However, as a general rule, the more officials know about the problems they face, the better equipped they are for addressing them.

Herbert Simon (1957) brings out an important fact related to the growing requirement for knowledge. He notes that burgeoning information flows simultaneously in all directions. Executives should be prepared to intercept that information at strategic points, hopefully before the problems cause havoc. Of equal importance, information usually changes constantly, altering its character in the process. Decisionmakers then must view information as a dynamic and not as a static source of knowledge. Accordingly, they have to test it and its sources periodically (pp. 167–169).

PERCEIVED IMPORTANCE OF PROBLEMS

One scholar has cited several representative factors that help determine the importance of problems (Janis, 1989, pp. 140–148). These include the relationship to vital interests, the linkage to acknowledged threats, the number of problems already on the agenda, the ambiguity of warnings, the gradual or precipitous growth of the problem, the vividness of its warning, and the sense of control that viewers feel they have over events. The perceived importance of an issue helps shed light on how one responds to a situation. For example, Admiral Husband Kimmel's failure in decision-making preceding the Japanese attack on Pearl Harbor can be explained by his perception of the importance of the situation. He certainly faced a question of decision avoidance. In many respects he was dammed if he did and dammed if he didn't. Given the size of the debacle, one certainly can conclude that the admiral failed to recognize the dimensions and gravity of the problem. With the aid of hindsight, we can see that he lacked vital information and failed to take important steps.

It is well known that because executives might recognize numerous problems and opportunities, they have to appraise each situation and assign priorities (Alden, 1997). In so doing, they typically have considered the following factors:

- *The extent of visibility.* Not all executives can see deeply into problems; this interferes with their efforts to solve them.
- *Source of pressure.* A variety of persons and organizations, both within and outside organizations, make demands on those investigating situations.
- *Personal interest.* Observers bring with them their own intellectual baggage and individual experiences, and these color their thinking.
- *Value to the organization.* Executives should be able to determine how important different situations are to the organizations they guide and direct.
- *Ease of solvability.* How executives view a problem is influenced by the intellectual effort and the resources needed to remove an unwanted situation.
- *Imminence of deadline.* The time in which executives must act influences how they view a particular situation.

Of special importance here, the prisms that executives use cause them to differ in determining which of these factors should receive the priority.

CHANGING NATURE OF PROBLEMS

Two examples illustrate that some situations, along with their problems, can remain stable for remarkably long periods of time. The British fleet ruled the waves from the time of Queen Elizabeth I until World War II. Since 1688, Lloyds of London has focused on the international insurance business. Since its earliest days, the company had recognized that one of its chief and abiding problems pertained to preventing its underwriting members from engaging in financial skulduggery.

As already noted, by and large, the character of problems facing any organization does not remain the same forever. An initial picture might hold true for a time, only to become invalid or different at a later date. Over its lifetime, even Lloyds of London has witnessed a series of changing problems. For example, not until 1982 did Parliament pass a new constitution aimed at preventing conflicts of interests that had plagued the company and the industry for three centuries. As a rule, decisionmakers cannot indulge in a one-shot investigation of a situation. No single look at reality remains valid for all time and under all circumstances. Therefore, as suggested earlier, in most cases a need exists to reevaluate periodically. One of the tasks of effective leadership is to indicate the changes that will improve the performance of an organization (O'Toole, 1995, pp. 12–13).

Romney to the Rescue

What actions might flow from asking, "From whose perspective?" The formation and wording of a problem often condition the responses of individuals or groups. We see such changing actions in the strategies developed by George Romney when he was president of American Motors Corporation (AMC). During the 1950s, American Motors adopted three different strategies based on its assessment of key problems associated with changing market challenges (Christensen et al., 1978, pp. 143–178).

During these years, given the growing competition of the three big automobile manufacturers—General Motors (GM), Ford, and Chrysler—AMC accurately recognized its key problem as survival. Romney saw no need for AMC to dominate the field. In fact, AMC didn't have the resources to accomplish this feat. Instead, Romney opted to capture a sufficient share of the market in order to make his firm profitable. The company adopted a "campaign for a survival strategy" (Christensen et al., 1978).

American Motors came into existence in 1954 through the merger of Nash and Hudson, both failing firms. In September 1954, sales had fallen off by some 42 percent from the preceding year. The company lost about $11.5 million. In three succeeding years, AMC's market share fell by a whopping 25 percent. Losses for these three years amounted to $15.2 million, $32.4 million, and $11 million, respectively. AMC reluctantly had to borrow heavily from several banks. Business reporters began writing obituaries for the firm's demise.

Having defined the problem correctly, AMC sought to remedy it by marketing its compact car. AMC expended considerable effort to convince its dealers and the public to buy this smaller version. Romney's efforts had spectacular results. By the end of 1960, the firm's sales had soared some 300 percent, its market share had tripled, and the company had an operating profit of $105 million. Although AMC continued to manufacture big cars, it took the lead among American companies in the sale of small cars.

In an unwise decision, the "Big Three" automobile manufacturers decided to produce larger, medium-priced cars. American Motors's equivalent cars, the Nash and the Hudson, could not compete. On the basis of this assessment, Romney decided to follow "a campaign of opportunity." AMC stopped producing the Nash and Hudson and made the historical decision to place all its chips on the Rambler, its compact car.

Not surprisingly, Ford and GM followed with their own compact cars. In 1961, Romney and his management team carefully reexamined the problem, concluding that the fierce competition among compact cars would continue as the most serious problem. What's more, this increasing rivalry would take place in a static automobile market. More and more people were replacing cars, not buying additional ones. Under such circumstances, a company's share of the market could grow only at the expense of the other companies.

In 1961, Romney successfully faced the counterattack campaign of Ford and GM. AMC redesigned the Rambler and introduced the popular hard-top models. It also made engineering changes in its larger Classic and Ambassador models. Rambler remained the leader in the compact car market, then the fastest-growing segment in the United States. Finally, AMC also launched major sales campaigns overseas in 1962.

This case illustrates clearly the changing nature of the problems facing executives. In the case of AMC, over the years, its leaders ably recognized the changes in the character of its major problems and acted accordingly. AMC survived during a stressful period in which other car firms floundered. Romney was successful because he expended efforts repeatedly to detect AMC's key problem and then to shift the company's corporate strategy accordingly.

Amdahl Episode

Differing points of view came into play when Amdahl (a computer company) and Dresser (an oil field hardware company) concluded major transactions involving the transfer of technology from the United States to foreign countries. In the post–World War II period, International Business Machines (IBM) dominated the world market for mainframe computers. In 1970, Gene Amdahl left IBM and set up his own company. Amdahl brought with him considerable technical knowledge, especially about the manufacture of large-scale, general-purpose mainframe computers (Baranson, 1978, pp. 75–84).

Amdahl had designed a new computer that used the most modern, large-scale integration (LSI) and created a computer-aided design (CAD) that resulted in much faster and more compact machines. Because of its LSI technology, Amdahl's computer would occupy only one-third the floor space of an IBM computer and realized cost savings of up to 50 percent (Baranson, 1978). Amdahl required additional financing but could not find any American investors. Desperate for funds, he signed a technology-sharing agreement with Fugitsu, a Japanese electronics firm. Over the years, as he borrowed more and more money, he increasingly transferred technology to Fugitsu. In time, the Japanese firm acquired enough new technical knowledge to enable it to enter the market in a competitive way.

Transferring technology to Fugitsu did not constitute a major problem to Amdahl because he was completely dependent on the Japanese firm for survival. Remember, he had no other source of funds. Moreover, participating with Fugitsu constituted an attractive way of bringing his new computer to the market. To IBM and to the rest of the American computer industry, however, Amdahl's actions presented a major problem. The industry estimated that the infusion of Amdahl's technology had allowed Fugitsu to close about a three- to five-year gap with U.S. industry. American computer firms now faced stiffer competition from Fugitsu.

Dresser Episode

The second episode relates to how some influential government officials and leaders in private industry differed about the question of technology transfer. Taking place during the height of the cold war, the case illustrates government's role in regulating the export of technology that might adversely affect the national security of the United States (Praskash and Ryan, 1979). With the end of the cold war, the question of technology exports to Russia no longer constitutes a major national security problem.

The issue arose when Dresser attempted to sell the Soviets information about manufacturing high-quality drilling bits. In March 1978, Dresser signed a contract to export such knowledge to the Soviet Union. Critics denounced the sale, arguing that the United States should deny the Soviet Union this technology to demonstrate its displeasure over Soviet violations of human rights. At first, the U.S. Department of Commerce approved an export license. Although the U.S. Department of Defense initially agreed, certain members of Congress, some industry executives, and high-level officials within the national security structure of the United States objected strongly.

Those who wanted to block the sale charged that the knowledge of this technology existed only in the United States. The USSR would have to come to American industry if it wanted this technology. By assisting the Soviet oil drilling effort, the United States would be helping an adversary gain economic strength, providing the Soviets with resources that they could use to increase their military strength. Critics loudly charged that the sale would prove inimical to the interests of the United States (Borchrave and Ledeen, 1980, pp. 13–17).

Dresser responded that it depended upon exports for much of its business, and the U.S. economy required exports to meet a serious balance-of-payments problem. Dresser disputed the argument that only the United States enjoyed this technology and contended that foreign companies also had this technology and could make a profit by selling it to the Soviets. Such a sale would not necessarily adversely affect U.S. national security. Just as important, Dresser's spokesmen contended that technology exports should not be used for "leverage" in foreign policy. The Carter administration postponed final approval of the Dresser sale and later announced that the Dresser factory would not be built in the Soviet Union.

Both parties asked the same serious question: "Would the sale be good for us or bad?" It seems that Dresser's top executives saw the problem as, "Would this sale to the Soviet Union prove advantageous to our firm and not inimical to the interests of the United States?" They answered "yes." Critics of the sale, on the other hand, viewed the problem as, "Would this sale to the Soviet Union have no harmful consequences for the national security of the United States?" They answered "no." Because the parties to the sale saw the problem differently, it is no surprise that they responded differently to this proposed technology transfer.

SUMMARY

This chapter examined one key point: From whose perspective is a problem being viewed? As indicated in this discussion, people can view the same set of circumstances differently. Any understanding of a problem cannot be complete or even sufficient unless it addresses and, hopefully, reconciles the question of perspective. The chapter illustrated how opposing views play themselves out in a number of different narratives such as Tanaca, the Osirak raid, Romney's leadership of AMC, and Amdahl's and Dresser's attempts at technology transfer. Through these discussions and case analysis, the chapter demonstrated the inevitable fact that various people can see the same information base in diverse ways.

CHAPTER 6

Critical Factors

This chapter focuses on certain critical factors that executives encounter when they tap information bases looking for problems. To gain an understanding of this subject, it is first necessary to note that just a century ago our predecessors addressed problems differently than we do today. Executives in contemporary times, in large part, have available to them analytical instruments that did not exist in the past. In the future they will have even better tools. They should not try to do tomorrow's job with yesterday's tools (Jun and Storm, 1973). This exhortation applies to efforts that executives make to remedy difficulties confronting them.

CONCEPTS OF TAPPING INFORMATION

Executives have to pierce formidable barriers that often surround information bases. This fact will not change much in the future. However, no doubt, the presence of the new analytical tools mentioned previously will alter how analysts perform this task. We can visualize their need to plunge conduits through rugged coverings enclosing information reservoirs and then siphon pertinent data to where they are needed (Kaplan, 1964).

Information also can be viewed as ore, which executives (like miners) dig, refine, and transform into a usable commodity. Another way of viewing this process is by comparing it to osmosis in living cells. Between the investigator and pertinent items within the information base lies a "semipermeable membrane." Analysts have to penetrate that membrane, strike relevant information, and then direct it through the porous membrane to executives who use it to make policy or to take other actions.

Facts and data often can remain so well hidden within a chaotic information base that they yield very reluctantly to even intensive interrogation. Disorder and confusion sometimes effectively resist the application even of logical interrogation methods. This chapter explores how executives go about pinpointing hidden facts or data and then attempt to see that the data flow, in an appropriate manner, to decisionmakers. It pays to repeat the suggestion that executives should try to bring order to any random conglomeration of facts and figures that they find.

Those looking for answers have to apply a "decisionmaking stethoscope" to discover vital signs within a "body" of information. One can liken an information base to the chest: both emit certain "sounds." As a physician can "read" these sounds by using a stethoscope, an executive can gain information from "information detecting instruments," such as documents, tables, calculators, and computers. By using these devices, executives can discover whether the data located in an information base are sound.

Executives sometimes interview their employees or customers to discover bothersome conditions. Small-business people query their cash register at the end of every day to learn the status of their sales. On the other hand, abiding problems prompt executives to undertake periodic and special studies. For example, the financial catastrophe that plagued many American savings and loan companies in the early 1990s triggered a spurt of large-scale analyses that examined the inimical forces that took a heavy toll of the nation's savings and loan community.

This chapter specifically examines certain key traits associated with information bases. These affect the way in which executives meet their responsibilities. They include (1) certainty and doubt, (2) complexity and simplicity, (3) surprise, and (4) urgency.

CERTAINTY AND DOUBT

Obviously, the more certain executives are about facts, the more likely they believe that they can successfully identify problems. To decisionmakers, facts represent evidence, which, if reliable, can convince them that they face truly unwanted conditions. As this study has emphasized repeatedly, executives must shift the nature of their information from "mixed up" to "well ordered," because logically arranged information tells them more clearly just how difficult a situation is.

It is worthwhile repeating that more than any other trait uncertainty makes the task of identifying problems difficult. Robin Hogarth (1987, p. 190) concludes, "Most decisions are subject to uncertainty." He continues that it is important to identify and quantify them. We often use the terms *likely, possible,* or *probable* to indicate that a problem has less than a 100 percent chance of either being discovered or solved, or both.

We also are aware that at times decisionmakers make choices with only partial knowledge, so-called educated guesses. Under conditions of uncertainty, decisionmakers obviously must estimate what might happen because they don't have all the facts. When asked to choose between two different descriptions of a situation, decisionmakers naturally try to select the one in which unsatisfactory circumstances seem closest to reality.

Hogarth also emphasizes the well-known fact that analysts use probability in their attempts to come to grips with doubtful problems. Earlier in this work, the language of expressing likelihood received attention. At this point, this study suggests how probability serves to (1) offer a common language for describing problems that experience unreliable traits and (2) provide a way of manipulating events (Turban, 1988, pp. 412–414). Even with the most effective quantitative techniques, however, one seldom can eliminate uncertainty altogether. Truth is often illusive, and people have to learn to operate in an incomplete and inexact world.

Furthermore, a less than fully understood situation obviously poses a great challenge to those seeking to comprehend it (Tuma and Reif, 1980). People sometimes gain reputations by attaining favorable results despite not understanding the tasks that confront them. Hernán Cortés's capture of Mexico's Aztec empire ranks as one of the most successful enterprises in history for that very reason. The Spanish conqueror arrived in Mexico in 1519 with only 600 soldiers and sailors, a very small (but well-trained) military force. At first glance, this force seemed too tiny to enable Cortés to capture Montezuma's vast empire. He did this by taking advantage of a political crisis in the Aztec empire, gaining thousands of Indian allies, learning the personality foibles of his chief enemy (Montezuma first thought that Cortés was the departed god Quetzalcoatl, who returned to Mexico from the East) (de Madariaga, 1948, pp. 48–49), and conducting highly intelligent military operations.

COMPLEXITY AND SIMPLICITY

Complexity also acts as a bothersome barrier to understanding problems. "Complexity and change," David Alberts and Daniel Papp tell us, "are the two defining characteristics of the Information Age" (1997, p. xvii). Logic tells us that it is easier to point out a whole composed of fewer parts than one containing many. We can comprehend complexity or simplicity best by citing the number of parts that constitute a fact or a problem. Simple phenomena have few interactive parts; complex phenomena have many. In the nineteenth and twentieth centuries, the world witnessed a strong trend toward larger scale and more complexity in its hardware, institutions, and administrative practices. People erected the tallest buildings, built the biggest ocean liners, and formed huge private companies and gigantic public agencies, each comprising numerous, interacting components.

As society increased the size and complexity of its technology and organizations, it also encountered more complicated problems of larger dimensions. To solve the problem of putting a man on the moon, scientists, engineers, managers, and executives at NASA had to identify and solve a huge number of major problems, requiring the application of many expensive resources. For example, hundreds of people in many industries and companies worked many hours to (1) build a heat shield that would protect the spacecraft during reentry, (2) acquire an inertial guidance system, (3) fashion a reliable communications system, (4) prepare the astronauts both physically and emotionally for the voyage, (5) construct a livable environment on board the spacecraft, and (6) perform other necessary technical feats.

People habitually prefer to face simple problems rather than the complex kind. If a youth lacks transportation to a nearby school, his parents solve the problem easily by getting him a bicycle. That solution makes individual transportation feasible. On the other hand, if pupils must travel many miles (as in the case of consolidated schools in rural areas), the community generally provides a more complicated transportation system, including buying and servicing buses, developing safety standards, training and certifying drivers, acquiring and maintaining equipment, and scheduling routes.

In certain important fields, the recent trend toward increased complexity has abated. For example, early business machines contained a large number of moving parts. Modern calculators using electronic chips are much simpler, smaller, less expensive, and more reliable and can do more work faster than their predecessors. Today's solid-state watches have fewer parts than the intricate Swiss watches of yesterday, but they keep time as accurately with no need for upkeep or adjustment. Exxon now sells the "Qyx," a new typewriter that operates with only a handful of moving parts compared to the old IBM Selectric. The Japanese now produce the Canon AE-1 camera with 300 parts fewer than the model it replaced. On the other hand, fashioning a simple design to address widely varied problems is enormously difficult (Edwards, 1984). Well into the future, executives are going to have to make judgments about how simple or complicated they can fashion their decisionmaking tools. Their conclusions, no doubt, will help model how executives direct their enterprises.

SURPRISE

No aspect about information bases frightens decisionmakers more than surprise. Executives hate surprise, especially of the unpleasant variety and the kind that occurs too late for them to take remedial action. How many times does one hear a deeply troubled executive lament, "If I only had known in time." Most well-trained and experienced executives work hard at discovering which problems to avoid. They pride themselves on their ability to detect warning signals in time. To them, the unexpected usually brings with it more difficult problems. Obviously, those executives who can anticipate or outguess unforeseen outcomes possess the qualities that firms or agencies like to see. After all, those in charge of information bases have the responsibility of keeping executives up to date. Surprise prevents executives from taking proper actions. What's more, they often have to take action in a race with time.

Let's look at some cases that illustrate the effects of surprise on identifying problems, decisionmaking, and on assessing outcomes: (1) farm tractors, (2) the Recording Instruments Corporation, (3) laboratory administration, and (4) the Cuban missile crisis.

Farm Tractors

Executives responsible for directing U.S. foreign assistance programs at times experienced unexpected problems with tractors that the United States had supplied to developing societies. By and large, administrators knew about crops, seeds, the use of fertilizers, the availability of water, and how farmers get their crops to market. U.S. agricultural experts tended to pay close attention to statistics illustrating per acre farm production and to average rainfall and temperature.

On the other hand, it seemed that U.S. officials tended to ignore critical social factors having relevance for farm technology. They often learned about the sad fate of tractors that the United States had given to underdeveloped countries from its technical experts visiting recipient countries. These professionals unexpectedly would see unused tractors rusting in the fields. Without technical training, peasants obviously did not know how to use this machinery. They lacked the skills to become competent tractor drivers and especially repair mechanics. The first time that a tractor broke down and peasants could not fix it, they abandoned it where it stood. The tractor remained idle and became subjected to the corrosive effects of weather. These abandoned vehicles unfortunately advertised to the world that the United States could not administer its foreign assistance programs properly.

Recording Instruments Corporation

The Recording Instruments Corporation (RIC), a small company founded in 1958, experienced surprise with the information it received. The company produced electronic instruments, such as a null-seeking servo-type plotter with X-Y coordinates, geophysical instruments, and electronic recording equipment (Bennett, Brandt, and Klasson, 1974, pp. 306–315). Lacking sufficient capital in its formative years, the company solved its plant space problem by leasing facilities in Los Angeles. RIC assembled products from purchased components. Because of the erratic performance of its new recording instruments during tests, the company unexpectedly judged that these items suffered major unknown problems.

The company sought to build an export trade with Europe. Edwin Ward, the company's CEO, belatedly learned of technical difficulties from the firm's agent in France who served an important client, the Parisien Institute. To their amazement and dismay, RIC's executives, who always prided themselves on their expertise in the field, began to hear customer complaints about receiving low-quality products. Buyers also complained about the aesthetics of the design.

Ward expressed surprise that some of the people on whom he had relied were concealing defects that outsiders discovered, causing him unanticipated embarrassment. He complained that the company's employees failed to give proper attention to detecting critical details and to adhering to exact specifications. He suggested that a real estate company might be able to get away with such sloppy performance but not a company manufacturing modern instruments. Ward called on his people to conduct careful analyses, schedule more tests, correct false information in its manuals, and above all, bring this information to the attention of decisionmakers in a clear and timely way. He argued that a firm that had built excellent prototypes should be able to transfer that excellence into production and not be surprised by low-quality products.

Laboratory Administration

Some time ago the following case (using fictitious names) made the rounds of schools of business administration. It illustrated surprise by an executive directing a research and development establishment.

Douglas Green, the head of a laboratory group in a large enterprise, was elated because his laboratory had achieved some notable recent success. People looked up to him as a dynamic head of an up-and-coming laboratory. Green especially took great pride in his recent promotion.

One evening, when Green stayed late to review the events of the day, a young man entered the laboratory. The man introduced himself to Green as William Schuster. Although disturbed by this intrusion, Green responded to his visitor pleasantly. In a highly pitched voice Schuster told Green that Thomas Elliot, chief of the division, had suggested that he visit Green's laboratory. On its face, this explanation for Schuster's appearance at the laboratory seemed to make good sense. Yet, in the back of his mind, Green wondered if Elliot was thinking about replacing him and preparing Schuster to take over his job. Worst of all, Elliot had told Green nothing about personnel changes. Green immediately began to worry.

Early the next morning Green trotted into Elliot's office and asked his boss about Schuster's status. Elliot replied that the firm's decisionmakers were thinking about hiring Schuster. The newcomer enjoyed an excellent record at a number of neighboring laboratories. Elliot had heard that Green was highly intelligent and a very able researcher. While the company was deciding where to place Schuster, Elliot thought the new man could learn most by working with Green's group. Green replied that he would welcome Schuster to his laboratory. He did not voice that already he had begun to fear that the young "genius" would attempt to take over the group.

Green introduced Schuster to the other members of the group; the new arrival seemed to strike up a close relationship only with George Senior, the group's mathematician. Green became increasingly disturbed as Schuster began to have more and more separate meetings with Senior. Yet he realized that Senior and Schuster shared a deep interest in quantitative methods. Nonetheless, as Schuster and Senior began to take over much of the group's discussions, Green became nervous and was afraid to disagree with Schuster in front of the group.

At one meeting, the group discussed a problem that it had concluded was impossible to solve. Schuster took this conclusion as a challenge and immediately went to the blackboard and showed how the group might attack this "impossible" problem. The reports about the man's capabilities seemed correct.

Later Green reluctantly withdrew his name as a candidate to give an important briefing to some visitors, suggesting that Schuster should present it. Schuster did very well, and that made Green even more uneasy. A number of attendees gathered about Schuster, praising him for his presentation and pumping him with questions. After that event, Green secretly started to look around for other employment and soon found an appealing job nearby. Green notified Elliot by direct mail. A short time later, out of the blue, Schuster also informed Elliot that he had accepted a more attractive offer from another laboratory and would leave in two weeks.

Elliot was surprised, shocked, and angry on learning that two of his prized laboratory directors were departing. Elliot already had decided to place Schuster in charge of a completely different project that had great need for someone with the man's talents. He especially felt betrayed because neither researcher had informed him of any difficulties in the laboratory that might have led to their decisions to leave. If he had known, he might have been able to take remedial action. After Green left, the laboratory was hard hit and, in fact, never recovered. George Senior was unable to lead the laboratory group effectively.

This case illustrates what happens when a boss is caught by surprise. The major problem never appeared in Elliot's information base. Neither Green nor other group members put it there. In fact, Elliot worked under the impression that things were going well.

How could Elliot have learned earlier about troubles in the laboratory? Should Elliot have notified Green at the outset that Schuster eventually would work in a different laboratory? Should he have emphasized that Schuster was working with Green's group solely to gain experience within the company? In the end, surprise caused both Elliot and the company to suffer a major loss.

Cuban Missile Crisis

No episode in modern history involved a problem more replete with dangerous surprise than the Cuban missile crisis of 1962 (Allison, 1971, pp. 102–117). This crisis grew out of the Soviet's clandestine introduction of strategic nuclear offensive missiles into Cuba. By the summer of 1962, U.S. strategic experts knew that the Soviets were supplying Cuba with a number of major weapons, including defensive surface-to-air missiles (SAMs). Agents and refugees also circulated unconfirmed reports that the Soviets had begun installing strategic offensive missiles on the island. The Soviets would take the serious risks of introducing offensive missiles there only to shift the nuclear balance to their favor.

In order to achieve the same strategic advantage that building missiles in Cuba would produce, the Soviet Union would have to spend billions developing large-scale weapons and deploying them elsewhere within the Soviet world.

Largely because the United States lacked concrete proof, it took no overt action against these purported deployments in Cuba. However, in October 1962, persistent reports prompted U.S. intelligence agencies to increase surveillance flights over the island. The United States sought information relating to two critical problems. First, U.S. leaders wanted to know if the Soviets really had introduced offensive missiles into Cuba. Second, if the Soviets were constructing missile sites, the United States had to know the rate at which these missile sites were becoming operational. Once these missiles became operational, they became an immediate threat against U.S. cities and the nation's nuclear forces (McNeil, 1982, p. 368). At the same time, an operational Soviet missile force in Cuba would have greatly reduced the policy options open to U.S. leaders.

On October 14, 1962, a U.S. high-flying U-2 spy plane discovered ballistic launching sites at San Cristóbal. This intelligence provided incontrovertible evidence. Shocked, President John F. Kennedy and his top aides began 13 of the most tense and momentous days in modern history (Kennedy, 1985). The White House identified the essential problem as the need to prevent the Soviets from gaining a major strategic advantage. It sought to accomplish this end by choosing a counteraction that would not trigger a nuclear war, which could bring disaster to the U.S. homeland, injure its allies, or endanger the whole world.

After intensive deliberations with his aides, Kennedy issued an ultimatum to the Soviets to withdraw the offensive missiles from Cuba. He placed a naval "quarantine" in the Caribbean, one that would prevent Soviet vessels from bringing more missiles into the island (the United States used the label "quarantine" rather than "blockade" in order to avoid certain difficulties in international law) (Palmer and Colton, 1984, p. 917). American leaders used the photographic evidence to convince the United Nations, the NATO powers, and other countries that the United States had good reason for its actions. As events proved, the naval quarantine induced the Soviet leader, Nikita Khrushchev, to back down and to consent to withdrawing the missiles. For its part, the United States promised not to invade Cuba.

Although applauding the final outcome of the crisis, many critics charged that the Soviet Union had inflicted a humiliating strategic surprise on the United States. The country's intelligence agencies came under fire for putting the nation in great peril by failing to acquire the information about the offensive missiles sooner. For his part, President Kennedy believed that he had to wait until he had absolute evidence (Divine, 1971).

URGENCY

Some problems demand immediate attention. An urgent problem naturally requires decisionmakers to apply their intellectual resources and investigatory powers as quickly as possible (Fink, 1986). In crisis situations, executives require those responsible for gathering information to inform them as rapidly as possible.

In November 1987, Ingersoll-Rand (IR) of Athens, Pennsylvania, became acutely aware of an urgent problem (Peters, 1992, pp. 72–85). Its cyclone grinder, an air-powered hand tool used for material removal and fine finishing, had become less creative, more expensive, and more time-consuming than earlier models. Dick Poore, sales and marketing vice president for IR Power Tool Division, told Jim Stryker, the marketing manager, to do something about the sagging grinder and to do it fast. To indicate the urgency of this effort, the company called it "Project Lightning." Stryker succeeded in fixing the problem swiftly. By January 1988, he had produced a highly marketable item, a commendable achievement. He did this, in part, by keeping his subordinate's feet to the fire while allowing slack at critical moments. Although the final outcome was favorable, the company should never have found itself in such a position in the first place.

On the other hand, some problems are less pressing. If decisionmakers believe that no urgency exists, they can take actions that cause delays in an undertaking. The courts seem to have concluded that they can slow down projects that might affect the environment adversely. For example, the Alaskan pipeline was delayed by court injunctions when the oil companies failed to demonstrate adequate protection of the environment (Sax, 1971).

LEAD TIMES

Most often, the timing of events can have an impact on the nature of problems. The question of urgency depends heavily on timing. We know that time is simply a duration. People commonly measure it by numerical units from seconds to millennia. In terms of the relationship between problems and time, executives have to concern themselves with such questions as: (1) When does an unsatisfactory situation initially exist? (2) When do executives first discover its existence (and what leads them to discover it)? (3) How long does it take for executives to understand the full or exact nature of a problem confronting them? (4) How long will the problem last? (5) When do the consequences of a problem begin to affect the executive who confronts it? (6) How long does it take for an executive to recognize those consequences? (7) How long does it take for executives to develop and implement counteractions or solutions to remedy those problems? Executives always seem worried about having enough time to make and implement decisions that would protect them and, hopefully, even improve their lot.

As the foregoing questions indicate, to perform in an adequate manner, executives not only must find the problems, but they must find them in time to take corrective action. The more complex and difficult the problem, the more time executives need to identify it, let alone solve it. This point needs no elaboration.

Problems that diffuse swiftly obviously demand that decisionmakers diagnose and prescribe for them quickly. Some authorities argue that no matter how efficient and well organized executives become, they almost never have enough time to do all that they want to do. Above all, in the minds of many, bureaucracies engage in time-wasting procedures and actions in seeking to detect and counter problems. For example, throughout large organizations some bureaucrats insist that every conceivable participant to a solution sign off (concur) on each issue addressed, thereby increasing in a major way the amount of paper and time needed to address a problem.

Stephen Andriole noted, "Like talent, data, methods, and approaches, time is a tool that must be used properly. Most importantly, it should be used to determine what can and cannot be attempted in a problem-solving situation" (1983, p. 19). When it comes to controlling time, executives would do well to conform to Aristotle's "golden mean." They should neither dawdle nor hurry. Yet at times they may find it necessary to go to extremes in very difficult situations, as Romney did when betting so heavily on the compact car.

One example gives insight about the relationship between time and problem recognition. New employees have to learn the location of various offices and facilities within a firm's physical plant. For the most part, the average worker gains this kind of information swiftly. There are times, however, when a recently hired employee takes an inordinate amount of time to gain this knowledge. Such lost time equals wasted resources. For this reason, many firms have established formal orientation tours to acquaint new people with the layout of a facility in the shortest time possible. It is routine for universities to organize such tours for freshmen, familiarizing them with the campus.

One's reputation for completing work on time often has a major impact on a business or public situation. In the mid-1970s, the French failed to sell their Mirage F-1 jet fighter to four small NATO countries (Belgium, Denmark, Norway, and the Netherlands). These NATO nations bought the American F-16 jet fighter instead. Granted, the allied nations selected the F-16 for a variety of reasons. Yet surely the French reputation for not delivering logistics support on time, although not the major reason, did contribute to the failure of the French to sell their aircraft. Here, a question of timing did take on importance. The United States enjoyed a considerable reputation not only for the high quality of its aviation hardware but also for the prompt delivery of logistic support to buyers (Leighton, 1976).

SUMMARY

This chapter focuses on how people go about discovering critical items contained in the information base. Executives must pierce that base if they want to get to information lying within. They require access to the types of information that will enable them to achieve their objectives. Awareness and cognition play critical roles in this endeavor. Obviously, in order for decisionmakers to get to know the problems requiring analysis, they should know exactly where in the information base the pertinent data or narrations exist. They also must become acquainted with those parts of the information base that describe the unsatisfactory conditions for which they are responsible.

This chapter presents an array of concepts for exploring the dynamics of problems. These concepts include certainty and doubt, complexity and simplicity, surprise, urgency, and lead times. Cases illustrating the dynamics and impact of surprise included (1) idle farm tractors (gifts of the United States) rusting in the fields of recipient societies, (2) the RIC story, (3) a sad saga in the field of laboratory management, and (4) the Cuban missile crisis of 1962. All the cases reinforced the idea that surprises result from deficiencies in the information bases of decisionmakers who may or may not have time to take remedial action.

CHAPTER 7

Hidden Information

Earlier I pointed out that problems sometimes are difficult to find in their information bases. In such cases executives might have to play the child's game of hide and seek. As in this game collectors conceal information or it inadvertently becomes hidden. Others have to locate it. Only investigators who have considerable talent, competence, and above all, persistence can find it.

Firms often try to keep information about new products hidden from public view. For one thing, commercial firms do not want competitors to know about the firm's problems. Of more importance, the more that industrial research and development create successful, new commercial products, the more competitors attempt to purloin proprietary information from leaders in the field. In recent years stealing secret data from competitors has become big business. Advancing technology, especially computers (including their software) and communication devices, has assisted in promoting the commercial espionage business. It also has prompted firms to install very expensive security systems designed to prevent such theft. Of course, nations have long operated spy services to ferret out useful information.

RELIABILITY OF INFORMATION

From time to time, the origins of information, especially that deliberately hidden from view, are not fully reliable. Above all, executives fear that questionable sources might supply them with distorted information. The results could cause trouble, even disaster. Executives want to prevent such consequences. Thus, they establish organizations that check on the accuracy of information and on the credibility of those who supply it.

National and military intelligence agencies try to use systems that indicate how much faith they can place in the data that their investigators, operatives, or spies dig up. In any intelligence situation decisionmakers always seem to deal with a mixture of evidence and inference. They have to reason from known or assumed facts in reaching firm conclusions. Just how much confidence can they have in their findings? The systems that they devise should answer this question in particular instances.

A hypothetical example will suffice here. Top officials might rank the validity of the information from A to D, with A meaning absolutely true; B denoting reasonably accurate; C signifying suspicious; and D pointing to totally false. They might rank the reliability of the source providing the information from E to H, with E denoting a highly trustworthy source, F a reasonably dependable supplier, G a questionable source, and H as totally unreliable.

We do not know if private industries as a practice have adopted such formal "ranking" systems. One might ask, Should they? After all, as has already been pointed out, the confidence that executives have in their information plays a crucial role in their decisionmaking. If collectors fail to establish confidence, the recipients might assume great risks. Discovering if businesses generally have adopted formal rating devices remains problematical.

Gillette's Intelligence Assessment

If executives must determine the validity of discovered facts, events, or numbers, they also have a responsibility to acquire and interpret that information in a way that favors the company's future. The case of the Gillette Company brings out the point that misinterpreting intelligence (usually gathered by marketing people) can have serious consequences (Gale, 1992, pp. 661–662).

During the 1980s, the top leadership of this company sought to improve its share of the market. On the basis of intelligence and the preferences of its executives, Gillette decided to emphasize the sale of inexpensive disposable razors over its traditional focus on selling a high-quality product. Disposable razors were priced at less than $2 per half-dozen as compared to the $3 and more for the Trac II and Atra shaving systems. The firm's officials thought that they had made the right decision when they put their eggs into the disposable razor basket.

To its dismay, the company's intelligence proved faulty. The firm lost many customers. It became clear that Gillette had made a major marketing mistake. At an earlier date, the company's advertising boasted that the Gillette razor offered the only way to get a decent shave. When Gillette concentrated on selling disposable razors, it hoped to pick up a share of a market that, at the time, seemed to have bright prospects. Apparently, Gillette's executives failed to explore deeply enough the question: "What does the information at hand tell us about the market potential for disposable products and what will happen to the company's ongoing sales strategy?" They apparently accepted faulty data or failed to identify the appropriate problem.

To Gillette's surprise, profits plummeted because consumers no longer considered high quality important. Increasingly, they bought throw-away razors. As consumers bought more and more cheap razors, the company, sensing its future at stake, became alarmed and took action to stop hemorrhaging profits.

In the 1980s, the firm responded first by taking over other companies that marketed products other than razors. Gillette's corporate leaders soon saw the futility in this strategy. The firm decided to go back to stressing a superior quality razor and developed the Sensor system. The Sensor's blades floated on tiny springs to conform more closely to the contours of the shaver's face. Initial sales exceeded expectations by some 30 percent. Gillette concluded that market specialists can create brand power and superior returns almost anywhere if only they focus on becoming perceived as high-quality leaders.

One can assess this case in terms of the importance of timing. In this episode, considerations of timing, although important, did not prove crucial. Officials at Gillette found enough time to develop new products and to place them on the market before earlier decisions inflicted mortal wounds. In this instance, response time favored Gillette, and the firm took advantage of it.

The Gillette case did not cite the specific financial burden that the firm incurred when reevaluating its position. However, most likely that cost was very high, especially when introducing Sensor technology or advertising for Trac-II or Atra razors. Fortunately, Gillette had asked itself: "Should Gillette go back to emphasizing high-quality products?" The firm returned to its old marketing strategy before too much elapsed time prevented it from catching up with competitors who had retained high-quality product lines.

ETHICS

The subject of espionage immediately brings up the subject of ethics. Gaining valuable information through immoral or unethical means can either benefit the culprit or vitiate the good that comes from such discovery (Sims, 1994). No doubt, companies have made effective use of information obtained in nefarious ways. Enjoying a robust economic boom at the end of the twentieth century, both Communist China and Taiwan have come to depend on the sales of their products to the United States. Yet their industrialists have illegally appropriated proprietary designs of American products without paying royalty fees. However, by violating proprietary rights, unethical Chinese businesspeople have exacerbated their relations with firms in the United States, at times losing opportunities for profitable cooperative ventures. For the most part, the Chinese seem willing to pay this penalty. Moreover, the diplomats of the two countries have had to spend a great deal of time and energy discussing this thorny topic.

Those who direct organizations know that they cannot impose absolutely rigid codes of conduct. If anything varies among humans, standards do. However, institutions can function in a tolerable way chiefly if their members do not deviate too far from commonly accepted notions of right and wrong. Competition in a society's economic sector does not justify a disregard for ethical behavior. The chief point here is that people should strive to build a society that rewards executives who adopt ethical ways of carrying on business.

Critics have condemned the ethics of certain bureaucratic techniques that organizations sometimes employ in dealing with information (Sanders, 1979, p. 7). In some cases top executives give subordinates insufficient time to conduct a thorough search and analysis. The initiator intends to exploit the "stampede effect," securing favorable action without having the matter undergo detailed consideration and evaluation. Subordinates are asked to reply in very short order (e.g., within 24 hours). Bosses simply do not give their people enough time to assemble and analyze the information that would support well-thought-through negative responses.

TYPES OF INVESTIGATION

It remains to explore the different ways by which executives interrogate problems that appear in their information bases. Before addressing specific types of investigation, however, we look at the role of identifying similarities and differences within the information base as well as the need to set boundaries around pertinent information pertaining to problems.

Similarities and Differences

It seems obvious that one should compare similarities and differences. If store owners see sales climbing but profits falling, they know that they have problems that can undo the good work of even competent sales personnel. They might suffer from poor accounting, inadequate and incorrect deliveries to customers, or runaway real estate or rental costs.

We can turn to the history of science to come up with needed insight into how similarities and differences affect information bases and thus help determine the fate of a company. In 1895 Wilhelm Roentgen, the German physicist, noticed that certain crystals had a fluorescent effect even through such material as a blackboard or thin sheets of metal. He knew that natural light could not produce this effect. Thus, Roentgen reasoned that a connection must exist between this effect and some new form of radiation. He called this discovery "X-rays" (radiation of very short wavelength). He reasoned that a link existed between radiation and the ability to penetrate opaque substances and affect a photographic plate. These discoveries originated because Roentgen sought to figure out similarities and differences in phenomena. X-rays differed from natural light in the ability to penetrate opaque substances. This discovery made possible new insights into the structure of matter and its relationship to energy. For his discovery, Roentgen won the first Nobel Prize awarded for physics.

Discovering identities and distinctions in the information base also can have a major effect on human endeavors, including that of industrialization. For example, Ransom Olds and Henry Ford saw that each worker could perform a different function instead of all doing similar steps. They appreciated an advantage in dividing a production process into a sequence of tasks (Rae, 1967, pp. 42–48). Before that time, each craftsman generally produced an article of hardware by completing all or most of the essential steps by himself. With each worker doing a specialized bit, the automobile factories of Olds and Ford could produce more cars at lower cost and in less time. In this case, these two men stood with the pioneers who introduced mass production and, thereby, helped create a new future for the industrialized world.

Boundaries

Another topic that merits attention relates to the role that boundaries play in gathering and analyzing information. Of great importance, the individuals assembling information and those analyzing it have to set limits. Borders restrict the dimensions of examination. For example, executives decide that certain elements of their organization should address problems having certain cost ceilings or floors (e.g., health care). Some staffs receive the authority to decide on programs costing $1 million or more; others are authorized to decide on programs involving less than $1 million. A company likewise designates the number of sales areas in each of its territories. This decision then determines the need for a certain number of salespeople and supervisors.

The boundaries of a problem have important consequences for decisionmakers now and in the future. Thus, decisionmakers might adopt specific approaches to help recognize types of problems. Boundaries become very important as they help establish the exact dimensions of the information task.

Estimates of the Situation

In approaching their need for information, executives have to assess existing combinations of circumstances in which they have an interest. For example, writers who have examined the role of executives in institutions aptly have named the stage just preceding decisionmaking "situational analysis" (Alden, 1994, pp. 1–9; Kepner and Tregoe, 1981, pp. 163, 184). At this point those who solve problems and those who make decisions have to size up the situation. This stage is influenced by the need to make two critical determinations: (1) recognizing that the need for a decision exists and (2) assessing the risks of avoiding a decision.

The situational analysis closely resembles the military's "estimate of the situation." The military profession has developed a method for determining precisely the situations that combat and support forces face (Ries and Trout, 1986). One confidently can liken the competition in the marketplace to armed conflict that takes place on the battlefield (Rogers, 1987). One should exercise caution before using military examples in deriving lessons about an executive's problems in the business world. Observers should move warily when comparing processes in different vocations.

On the other hand, the military's estimate of the situation clearly offers decisionmakers in a variety of institutions a powerful instrument for laying out problems. I commented earlier that perhaps more than any other professionals military commanders have to target their problems as precisely and clearly as possible. After all, they are responsible not only for the outcome of military operations but also for the lives and welfare of their troops. No wonder military establishments arose as one of the very first institutions to focus on designing an effective, systematic method for identifying problems.

Commanders call on their troops to collect, collate, analyze, and disseminate the information that they need for the conduct of military operations. Estimates of the situation consist of nothing more than statements of identified problems. From time to time, these estimates suggest solutions, but for the most part, they provide commanders with the natural obstacles and the forces that oppose them. It is in the higher echelons that most of this information is interpreted. Well-prepared commanders are acutely aware that the value of their information changes from time to time and from situation to situation. Accordingly, military staffs periodically review and revise these estimates.

In civilian life, executives also can design "estimates of a situation" to accomplish their own missions. In whole or in part, businessmen could portray germane information regarding their enterprises. Like military commanders, civilian executives often face a scarcity of talent. They can either forego certain kinds of information or widen the areas that each of their information sources has to cover.

Whether for the military or for industry, the estimate still performs largely the same function. It assists decisionmakers in learning the true facts about the situations that they face. It pays, then, to cite briefly the critical areas of these military estimates. They will help executives decide if, in any particular case, they can draw inferences for civilian enterprises.

CRITICAL AREAS

Military estimates emphasize the following major subjects:

* *Personnel.* The ability and preparation of military forces to achieve the major missions of the armed forces, including training and morale.

* *Intelligence.* The characteristics of the area of military operations and the disposition of enemy forces. The commander prefers that these estimates distinguish between physical conditions, such as climate, weather, topography, and geography.

* *Operations.* Estimates of how well various military forces interact with each other to carry out the mission of the total organization. This factor contains information about friendly and enemy military strategy, tactics, and operations. (From time to time this information might suggest possible courses of action available to the commander.)

* *Logistics.* Estimates of the resources and the ability of a commander to exploit them intelligently on the battlefield. Both the commander and the enemy will consider these resources as affecting the ability of each to fight.

* *Civilian-military.* Estimates of the treatment that military forces display toward varying types of civilians, including life or death situations. This type of information has very limited use in the commercial world.

One easily can perceive the civilian counterparts to these military areas (at least, associated with the first four). Just a few questions show the relevance: How can a company best inform itself about what to expect in the marketplace? Does the estimate accurately portray the behavior of competitors within a market economy? How well trained are the company's executives and workers compared to those of competitors? What is the situation in terms of the firm's ability to deliver parts and services? What are the financial and technological characteristics as well as the performance track record of certain executives or their companies, compared to those of others?

SEMANTIC LEADS

In order to find pertinent information, searchers using any system must look for semantic leads—key words or phrases that decisionmakers use in attempting to identify unsatisfactory conditions.

In seeking problems, decisionmakers must translate essential facts into a language that they and their audiences can understand. Semantic leads represent clues that executives find and follow in order to make problems meaningful. To do this, searchers look for "key words" or "descriptors." This process closely resembles the way in which operators in enterprises move beyond unrefined and undigested words and discover words that reflect meaning more precisely.

These words may be more or less comprehensive. As much as possible, the executive bears the responsibility for finding the most effective semantic leads. More precisely, descriptive leads usually enable searchers to discover more easily the exact problems that they want to find. For example, the word *transport* is less precise than the phrase *jet-powered 474 aircraft transport*. Likewise, using the word *crop* is less exact than the words *hard red winter wheat*.

Librarians know that the more exact the lead word, the easier for the searcher to gather the right information in a shorter time. Wrong or inaccurate lead words can saddle librarians with an illogical and sometimes massive mess. Put another way, when viewing the information base, decisionmakers simultaneously can face a prodigious feast or a serious famine of information, with the inevitable adverse consequences of each.

In most cases, the great challenge in identifying problems is to narrow the number of meaningful semantic leads to manageable levels. This task often asks much of an organization's executives.

LIBRARIES AND COMPUTERS

The task of investigating problems resembles a librarian's search for citations. The modern librarian relies on sophisticated computer systems to locate pertinent citations and to perform other practical applications.

Note that computers and their software can take the form of complex, rigorous processes. The arrival of the personal computer enabled librarians to work through terminals with a "user-friendly" (easy to operate) design. The shift to relatively small computers that could sit on table tops throughout the library enabled searchers to seek information anywhere and at any time. Libraries could imprint their entire catalogue of books, magazines, and other material on such computers. Libraries face the problem of using electronic systems to locate the necessary information at the right time (Evans, 1995, p. 4).

In a computer search, the investigator first attempts to identify all documents that contain a discussion of similar descriptors. In the initial search, the computer can reveal a data base ranging from almost no pertinent citations to one that literally overwhelms the searcher. The computer can spew out so much information that what was once a relatively easy chore, needing only the right words, becomes difficult. The searchers have had to come up with descriptors that most precisely relate to the problems under study.

Executives who want to compare analogies also can apply the same or similar library search techniques. With proper software, they can analyze analogous situations with no greater challenge than what librarians face today in their literature searches. In many instances, historical information stored in the mind enables decisionmakers or well-informed individuals to resort to analogies without requiring a computer. For example, President George Bush needed no computer to make the analogy between Iraq in 1991 and Germany at the end of the 1930s.

On the other hand, to come up with analogies associated with the information base (especially programs) might require the use of more advanced rigorous techniques. The mind often does not retain such data in a state of immediate recall. In these instances, executives must continue to document the information they find.

INFORMATION-PROCESSING DIFFICULTIES

Obviously decisionmakers prefer to apply reason in discovering abnormal and unsatisfactory situations within the information base. As competent individuals, they want to bring these facts to the attention of appropriate audiences as clearly and completely as possible. They do this by transmitting signals containing facts. From time to time communicators detect blockages, distortions, overloads, and especially noise that impede the proper transmittal of signals. *Noise* constitutes any unwanted electrical signal that interferes physically with the sound or image being transmitted. If such is the case, communicators say that there is static (or noise) in the circuit. In this context, static or noise limits the quality of messages.

Noise also relates to the introduction of signals representing words or thoughts that prove deliberately wrong, irrelevant, distorted, or misleading. Executives must determine whether these signals correspond to reality or to rumor, unsubstantiated charges, half-truths, or outright falsehoods. We hope that communicators can separate noise from valid signals. At times executives have to discover if the sender of information is attempting a cover and deception ploy (deliberate obfuscation and deceitful trickery). No matter what the name—static or noise—those relying on communications must take care not to become victims of static or misinformation.

Some individuals deliberately attempt to manipulate information to prompt the listener to arrive at incorrect conclusions. However, as a rule, people transmit correct information. In their daily operations executives in large-scale enterprises assume that they are receiving signals that clearly and unambiguously depict the true features of an entire problem. On the other hand, we already have noted that executives often operate with partial (and sometimes with complete) ignorance, and that fact makes them susceptible to unavoidable error or deliberate chicanery. However, a marked difference exists between honest mistakes and purposeful efforts to deceive. In addition, much of the time, decisionmakers have to rely on late or secondhand information.

Pearl Harbor

The inability of executives to differentiate between noise and fact can lead to intelligence fiascos. In her widely respected book assessing the Japanese attack on Pearl Harbor on December 7, 1941, Roberta Wohlstetter (1962) wrote about the difficulty of distinguishing noise from political and military hard facts. During the events leading to the Japanese attack, communications between U.S. leaders in Washington and military commanders at Pearl Harbor were unclear, inconsistent, and delayed. Admiral Husband Kimmel was receiving mixed signals about Japanese intentions and activities. He could not determine exactly what the Japanese were up to. As a result, the U.S. Navy at Pearl Harbor never really prepared for the Japanese assault.

In this case, top decisionmakers in Washington remained unaware of the real problem until the U.S. fleet lay in ruins. The Pearl Harbor episode illustrates a key point: Decisionmakers must try to ascertain the true message in time, no matter how much noise distorts a communication. They should have had available well-prepared experts who could separate noise from reality.

Lastly, despite the noise that might impede the communications system, people in charge of unsuccessful ventures often understand that critics will blame them for suffering an intelligence failure. This fact was pointed out earlier in the discussion of the Cuban missile crisis.

SUMMARY

The difficulties encountered in seeking out appropriate problems in an information base may be formidable, but certainly executives often can address this challenge effectively. Both governments and private firms search for appropriate and pertinent information, looking especially for trends. They look for facts, pursuing semantic leads that hopefully will prove precise. Organizations have fashioned various approaches to tapping the information base for pertinent data, including estimates of the situation, semantic leads, library searches, and distinguishing facts from noise in the signals emanating from the information base related to particular episodes. Although a number of approaches have been suggested here, in many cases, executives fashion their own analytical modes. The chapter ends with a discussion of the communications system during the Japanese attack on Pearl Harbor and how noise prevented higher decisionmakers from assessing the gravity of the situation. Ultimately decisionmakers must translate the essential facts within the information base into a language that they and their audiences understand.

CHAPTER 8

Skills

Alfred Schoennauer (1981, pp. 16–17) argues that problem finding requires different types of abilities than does problem solving. Executives might find it difficult to become proficient in both, but obviously knowing both helps executives. We do not know which problem-solving techniques might prove appropriate for finding a specific unwelcome situation. Up to now executives most likely have not given enough thought to developing and sharpening skills for problem recognition, a situation they should remedy.

CALLING SHERLOCK HOLMES

In one way or another, every book on executive decisionmaking exhorts readers to investigate their professional worlds closely. Executives should approach the task of discovering problems with the same enthusiasm as Sir Arthur Conan Doyle's legendary detective Sherlock Holmes brought to fighting crime. This sleuth displayed fully disciplined logic in responding to crime. One could say that businesses and public agencies could benefit today from a Sherlock Holmes approach.

In addressing problems, modern sleuths look for telltale clues that, hopefully, enable them to disentangle the trivial from the critical. Organizational detectives obviously are not always as successful as Sherlock Holmes. The idea of using one's intelligence to detect clues that lie hidden deeply within an information base and to understand their meaning should attract curious executives.

Above all, decisionmakers should have a firm idea of how to go about discovering serious lapses in performance. They can employ a number of functions (such as blockbusting) (Adams, 1979, pp. 1–11) that are designed to move beyond the obvious or even beyond the known. Even when the task of inquiry becomes routine and perhaps even dull (as often happens), no alternative exists to investigating the information base (Brownstone and Carruth, 1979; Scheffler, 1963). Theoretically, the number of relevant questions that bosses can ask is as vast as the number of people thinking about them. To keep the discussion within reasonable bounds, this study addresses only six considerations.

First, decisionmakers must take into account the extent and gravity of problems within their organizations. As a rule, they must decide which problems demand what priority. For example, in the late 1990s Bill Gates at Microsoft has had to pay more attention to antitrust matters.

Second, executives often have to respond to outside pressures. These pressures show up in information bases. For example, public pressure to preserve the environment has induced CEOs to pay more attention to ecological matters.

Third, if decisionmakers begin to take a substantial interest in an emerging problem, they inevitably assign increasing importance to it. The information base should reflect this shift.

Fourth, those in charge can focus their efforts either on the organization itself, on the members that comprise it, or on both. Those who focus on members will benefit if the information base adequately identifies members and their major traits.

Fifth, the more decisionmakers believe that they have to solve an emerging problem, the greater the chances that they will attempt to define the problem more precisely.

Sixth, the extent to which executives have access to resources determines how deeply they can tap the information base. In fact, access greatly influences whether executives even attempt to identify these problems, let alone try to solve them.

ARRAY OF SKILLS

The following sections explore five skills that help executives become proficient in problem identification: (1) mathematics, especially arithmetic, (2) common sense, (3) statistics, (4) analysis, and (5) priority setting.

Mathematics

Mathematics contains skills for addressing problems by organizing, simplifying, and interpreting data. Mathematicians perform calculations necessary in studying subjects in business, industry, and government. Problem identification techniques often require mathematical calculations.

Arithmetic is the branch of mathematics devoted to the study of numbers, relations among numbers, and the manipulation of numbers. We always seem to assume that every decisionmaker possesses the basic skills of addition, subtraction, multiplication, and division. With such proficiencies, people can do simple calculations, and in many cases, no more than arithmetic skill is needed for problem identification. In some instances rigorous analytical tools so mezmerized some executives and analysts with what advanced quantitative techniques can do that they ignored what simple arithmetic offered.

It should come as no surprise that problem identification also benefits from applying mathematics. Very often the trends and patterns within information bases that signify problems appear as numbers, and only by investigating these numbers can executives gain the truth. For this very reason, computers, which operate on numbers, have become indispensable in identifying unwanted situations.

Common Sense

In determining the components of the information base, bosses often seem to take great pleasure in exhorting subordinates to use their common sense. At times, less-educated executives and subordinates seem to wear "common sense" as a badge of honor, substituting it for formal analysis. Much can be said for such thinking. It is not just those familiar with rigorous analytical techniques who have the capacity to identify problems.

In applying common sense, decisionmakers use practical and ordinary intelligence or sound judgment based on actual experience to guide them through the mess that can characterize an information base. They resort to common sense because they cannot understand, or prefer not to expend the effort to learn, the often difficult-to-grasp concepts associated with advanced analysis. Moreover, they might believe that the use of rigorous techniques does not always, or often enough, get better results.

An important class of problems that at first seems suitable for a commonsense approach actually could benefit from rigorous analysis. Situations in which waiting lines occur are of the latter type (Knowles, 1989, pp. 789–792; Stevenson, 1989, pp. 663–669). Most of us frequently have to wait in line at supermarket checkout counters, at toll booths, and at gas pumps. It seems logical for those directing traffic to use platforms to service the delivery trucks that arrive first. "First in, first out" seems a logical way of doing business. As suggested, this way of doing things appears like a commonsense approach.

Yet common sense can fail us. A waiting line system has customers, a service facility, and a queuing discipline. Because machinery breaks down, because needed information can be missing, and because some employees can be unfamiliar with dock procedures, sometimes the queue discipline, the set of rules by which customers gain service, fails to function.

Inasmuch as trucks arrive at random intervals, the best way to load and unload the trucks might not follow a commonsense approach. Rigorous analysis (queuing theory) might show a better way. In the practical world, it could turn out that such a quantitative technique would prove a superior guide. It could show that "common sense" such as "first in, first out" may not be the most effective way to schedule waiting vehicles. Similarly, the owners of a new restaurant may want to know the size of the area to accommodate customers who are waiting to be seated (Stevenson, 1989). Rigorous analysis could tell the proprietors the number of customers waiting at a critical time.

Statistics

Executives very frequently use statistics in addressing problems (Kroeber and LaForge, 1980; McClave and Ditrich, 1983). Statistics involves collecting and analyzing data, and some consider statistics an applied science. This discipline offers a useful way for dealing with an adverse situation; sometimes it may be the only effective way (Blalock, 1960). The discipline of statistics is based on mathematical probability associated with idealized concepts of the subject (or model) under study (Stevenson, 1989).

In simple terms, a statistic is a measure, quantity, or value that often is calculated from a sample of an entire situation. Statisticians can make accurate estimates of an event on the basis of analyzing small samples. In practice, executives apply three types of statistics: (1) the rigorous and esoteric techniques associated with operations research, (2) simplified analysis, and (3) an improved form of presentation. This discussion is limited to types 2 and 3 because these are more frequently employed at the top levels of decisionmaking.

Statisticians can make as important a contribution to the success of a business or public organization (Spirer, 1975) as any analyst, accountant, or engineer (Lindsay, 1958, pp. 12–13). Even executives who have little or no knowledge of esoteric quantitative approaches can gain an adequate, and sometimes a clearer, understanding of an unsatisfactory situation. Of great importance, executives may find benefit in illustrative materials like graphs, tables, diagrams, charts, trend lines, and maps—all of which take a bit of statistical adroitness.

National leaders often use statistical displays at the highest levels of decisionmaking. In recent years, U.S. presidents have appeared on television to explain complicated socioeconomic problems. By showing statistical graphics, presidents were able to illustrate to huge television audiences that the national debt has been erased. Similarly, boards of directors of private companies periodically listen to status reports by the CEO presented in a statistical motif. It is well to reiterate here that good decisionmaking increasingly has come to depend on applying sound statistical approaches and presenting them with telling effect.

Analysis

Executives find that in order to identify a problem they have to separate or break up the whole of that problem into its parts. In so doing they apply analysis. They have to examine these parts to determine their nature, proportion, function, interrelationships, and the like. Researchers have applied an array of quantitative tools in performing this task (Churchman, Ackoff, and Arnoff, 1957). They have applied the quantitative approach in such areas as forecasting, budgeting, planning, scheduling, inventory management, and production (Stevenson, 1989, p. 4). In performing quantitative analysis, researchers often resort to using models to give them answers (Lave and March, 1975). However, although analysts have achieved major progress in applying their techniques, they still experience difficulty in dealing with the complexity of quantitative problem solving (Blalock, 1970).

Although computers and their software have lessened the dependency of executives on mathematics in making decisions, executives still often justify their decisions with quantitative analysis (Knowles, 1989, p. v). Inasmuch as analysts largely have neglected problem identification, they likewise have failed to fashion a significant number of quantitative techniques for this purpose. An in-depth examination of the use of quantitative analysis in problem identification lies beyond the intention and scope of this study. Hopefully, other books will appear in the future devoted to this specific subject.

Priority Setting

By setting priorities among various items within an information base, analysts should be able to improve their performance, especially in allocating resources (Steele, 1975, pp. 104–113). They naturally give more weight to some problems than to others. For example, most executives know from bitter experience that they find it difficult to abandon an item appearing in a budget for a long time, even if it is wrong, obsolete, or irrelevant.

Figure 8.1 charts an organization confronting three major hypothetical problems at the same time. To simplify this analysis, each problem comprises the same 10 deficiencies (or criteria). After a review, a CEO listed the following 10 deficiencies: an inadequate dress code for all employees; a reliance on outside contractors for supplying most parts and logistics

Figure 8.1
Problem Identification Comparison

Criteria	Analyst A	Analyst B	Analyst C
Dress code	10	10	10
Outside contractors	9	5	6
Outside interests	6	8	9
Faulty marketing	1	7	7
Becoming a conglomerate	7	1	1
Poor labor/management	3	6	5
Inadequate advertising	4	2	3
Poor locations	8	3	4
Hostile government policies	5	9	8
Faulty communications	2	4	2

support; too much interference from outside interests (e.g., stockholders); faulty marketing measures that distort demand; becoming a conglomerate by buying other businesses with different missions; poor relations between management and labor; poor and inadequate advertising; improper location of major facilities; hostile government attitudes; and faulty communications. The top executive then weighted these 10 deficiencies from the most serious (1) to the least serious (10). In order to determine the significance of these rankings, analysts compared each ranking against the others.

In Figure 8.1, the ranking of each criterion results from the subjective judgment of an analyst. The vertical ranking designates how an analyst compares the gravity of all 10 criteria, each against the others. Of course, if different analysts were comparing the same problem, the figure shows the ranking horizontally, indicating the variation among three analysts. For example, the first analyst might indicate a weight of 2 to the problem of faulty communications; analyst B might rate it with a 4; whereas analyst C might again give it a 2. In this case, all of the analysts considered the problem grave or serious.

On the other hand, the analysts disagree in a major way when viewing the problem of a firm becoming a conglomerate. Analysts B and C believed that the company being examined made a major mistake in acquiring other enterprises (giving it a 1); analyst A determined that this action had little impact (giving it a 7).

Analysts used subjective reasoning in determining all the weights in Figure 8.1. They have devised a few such quantitative methods for analyzing problem identification, including the Delphi technique. The latter is a method of making effective use of informed judgments of experts about the future. It tries to tap and evaluate expert opinion systematically (Helmer, 1967; Sanders, 1973, p. 297). Hopefully, future researchers will fashion others.

Choosing Severities

One other point about priorities deserves a comment here. Inasmuch as organizations recognize numerous problems and opportunities, they have to assess the challenge of each situation and assign appropriate priorities. Decisionmakers typically consider a number of factors in prioritizing unwanted situations. The extent of visibility is important because it helps determine just how clearly executives see a problem. The external and internal pressures that executives encounter also help them choose their priorities. Of course, each decisionmaker has his or her own personal interest. For instance, executives believing that organizations should use rigorous logic in addressing problems would give quantitative analysis a high priority. Of equal importance, the value of a certain problem to an organization should help determine its priority.

In coming up with priorities, organizations also consider the ease of solvability. As a rule, the easier a problem is to solve, the more likely analysts will give it a high number. Executives give problems having shorter deadlines a higher number. Very frequently institutions operating in a dynamic environment must come up with solutions at a moment's notice in order to survive.

ANALOGOUS REASONING

One skill that decisionmakers require—but that the literature often ignores or underrates—is the ability to discern a likeness between things that otherwise appear dissimilar (Neustadt and May, 1986, pp. 89–90). We call such a connection an "analogy." We can view an analogy simply as a comparison between events, ideas, or other things. It offers a helpful suggestion that decisionmakers can use in solving problems (Hogarth, 1987, p. 169) and in fashioning or justifying action. Above all, analogy offers a way of profiting from experience by determining the degree to which the past resembles or has relevance to a new situation. Decisionmakers look to the information base to see if analogies exist. Today analysts see an analogy between computers and the way that the human mind, and especially the memory, works.

The ability of executives to perceive an analogy depends on their capacity to retain information. To capture significance between the past and the present obviously demands that one keep in mind something once learned. People always have remembered information, but over the years, both government and private firms have expanded their sources and use of information. By now we all know that in addition to traditional sources of information (such as books, reports, newspapers, magazines, and journals) computers serve as a common means for storing data and disseminating such information.

Analogy has implications for all kinds of enterprises. Let us first examine the use of analogy by national governments and then see how commercial enterprises employ analogy in shaping business policies and practices.

Analogy in National Security

Leaders often resort to historical analogy, finding it a natural way to justify a course of action. National leaders employed analogies during the Persian Gulf War. As noted in Chapter 5, on August 2, 1990, Iraqi military forces invaded Kuwait, its neighbor to the south ("Iraq Army Invaded Capital," 1990, pp. A1, A8). President George Bush immediately condemned the invasion, calling it "naked aggression," the very words that the United States and the Allies used to describe Nazi Germany's invasions during the World War II period ("Iraq Forces," 1990, pp. 25–31). President Bush thus resorted to historical analogy in comparing Iraq's aggression to Adolph Hitler's. The United Nations Security Council also denounced the Iraqi attack in similar terms ("United Nations Condemns," 1990, p. A8). After Iraq captured Kuwait, the president ordered a U.S. military buildup in the Persian Gulf area and formed a coalition of like-minded nations to counter the Iraqi move.

American congressmen also make use of historical analogies. Several of them assailed Saddam Hussein, the Iraqi leader, as a madman and compared him to Adolf Hitler ("Senator Claiborne of Rhode Island," 1990, p. A8). U.S. leaders made it plain that to accept passively Iraq's aggression constituted nothing less than appeasement. In 1938 Great Britain and France caved in to Hitler over the Czechoslovakia issue in Munich (Palmer and Colton 1984, pp. 801–802). The failure to act against Germany came to be called "appeasement." Language such as this reminded the public that the failure to stop Hitler during the 1930s led to a subsequent costly and bloody war. In the Persian Gulf War, the coalition partners knew that if they failed to act against Iraq, they would be repeating this disgraceful chapter. They understood that they had to avoid another Munich. Saddam Hussein's aggression would not stop at Kuwait if he met no opposition there.

Iraq continued to hold on to Kuwait past the deadline established by the United Nations. On January 16, 1991, President Bush ordered air attacks against Iraqi military forces ("U.S.-Led Coalition Attacks Iraq," 1991, pp. 25–31). On February 23 the United States and its coalition partners launched a powerful ground assault, which by February 27 had completely routed the Iraqi armed forces ("Ground Attack Launched," 1991, pp. 125–126). President Bush also likened the Persian Gulf War to World War I, contending that the victory over Iraq was not waged as a "war to end all wars," as the Allies had advertised the war of 1914–1918 ("Cease-fire Holds in Persian Gulf," 1991, p. 156).

In formulating military strategy for the Gulf War, President Bush used another analogy. He said that the coalition partners would not liberate Kuwait by repeating the Vietnam strategy of a gradual military buildup over many years. In Vietnam, the United States raised its level of violence in response to the intensity of the enemy's military operations. Bush did not want to relive that problem. He knew that the strategy of gradualism had very nearly torn the American people apart. This time he wanted to assure the American public that the U.S. military would strike a very powerful blow against Iraq in order to knock Iraq out of the war in short order. He kept his word.

One can challenge the validity of using historical analogy to describe problems. After all, real differences exist between Hitler and Saddam Hussein. Hitler headed an industrially advanced country (manufacturing most of its own weapons) that had global ambitions; Saddam Hussein ruled a developing country (importing most of its weapons) and had regional aspirations. Nevertheless, meaningful historical similarities exist. Both Hitler and Saddam Hussein shared an appetite for power and aggression. This fact prompted both Bush and various congressmen to resort to historical analogy in their justification for attacking Iraqi forces in the Persian Gulf.

A critic also might argue that the American public did not really believe that the war in the Persian Gulf would end all possible future wars in the region. An objective observer might criticize Bush's statement as being superfluous. Any rational witness to the conflict would have to agree that Bush's stated strategy of applying overwhelming force at one time, in contrast to the gradual military buildup strategy in Vietnam, made good sense.

Historical analogy results from a decisionmaker's knowledge of history, not from some computer run. After all, President Bush did not consult computers in making the analogy between the Iraqi situation in 1991 and Germany's some 50 years earlier.

Analogy in Commercial Enterprises

By using analogy, top executives in private companies also can become more effective. Edwin Land, who founded the Polaroid Company, benefited from an analogy with Thomas Edison and his companies. Edison almost ruined his companies because he insisted on remaining the "boss" in each. Once his firms reached middle size, they were close to collapse. The firms saved themselves only by booting Edison out and replacing him with a professional manager.

Like Edison, Land ran his company tightly in its early, formative years. When Polaroid began to grow rapidly, Land sought to avoid Edison's mistake. He hired a new CEO, who set up a competent team to assist him. Together, they directed the day-to-day operations of the firm. Land restricted his own activities to the laboratory and to consultation on matters of basic research (Drucker, 1985, p. 202). He had learned a valuable lesson from Edison's mistake.

Southwest Airlines

The analogy approach was also useful in the airlines industry (Walden and Lawler, 1993, pp. 17–22). Since 1973, only one American airline, Southwest Airlines, has showed a profit every year. It based its success largely on modeling itself after Pacific Southwest Airlines, an intrastate airline limited to California. It avoided the errors of other airlines, which at first emulated Pacific Southwest's style of operations and then greatly altered and expanded their route structures, services, and equipment.

By imitating the mode of operations of Pacific Southwest Airlines, Southwest Airlines became very successful. It enjoyed a very good reputation in California for high frequency of flights, no gimmicks, no advance purchases, and very friendly personnel.

Using Pacific Southwest as its model, the Texas-based airline restricted its operations to (1) short-haul trips (less than 500 miles), (2) point-to-point flights rather than through-the-hub arrangements, (3) flying in and out of less-expensive, secondary airports (usually closer to the downtown area), (4) flying often and with little turnaround time (under the principle that aircraft on the ground do not earn money, (5) gaining economies by flying only one type of transport, the Boeing 737, and offering no fringes like airline meals, and (6) perhaps its most daring innovation, lowering fares from one-third to one-fifth of that charged by competitors. Executives at Southwest Airlines opted for simplicity in operations to gain these economic benefits. It since has spread its operations to several routes outside California but kept the original concepts.

The failure of other airlines that had started out earlier in the same mode as Pacific Southwest Airlines served as an analogy. The executives at Southwest Airlines never forgot that in the late 1970s U.S. Air purchased a successful Pacific Southwest Airlines, U.S. Air then added new routes and began to compete with other large airlines that also served these new destinations. As a result, it abandoned the very practices that had made Pacific Southwest Airlines a success and had to take major, costly efforts to extricate itself from some serious problems.

The Impact of Hindsight

Obviously, helped by hindsight, it is easier to assess why a particular solution had failed or succeeded. Hindsight tells the executive what should have been done. By using hindsight, critics have an easier time determining the policies and frames of reference for making difficult trade-offs. Executives often use hindsight in cases in which they made their original decision without considering some contingency that ultimately happened. Hindsight often involves the forgetting of known evidence, which executives later discover (Lindley, 1985, pp. 191–193). Unfortunately, at the time of an initial challenge, decisionmakers do not have hindsight available to them. Nonetheless, they still have to identify problems. The lessons of the past can help executives make present and future problem identifications. Executives will continue to use the hindsight approach, sometimes with little success but at other times with telling effect.

SUMMARY

In large part, the merits of decisionmaking depend on whether executives possess certain skills that determine the quality of their performance. They should behave like an organization's detectives who investigate troubling situations within that institution just as those on a police force try to solve crimes. These institutional "detectives" have to assess the gravity of problems, respond to outside pressure, assign importance to their work, focus attention on the members of the organization, believe in precise definitions, and rely on resources in order to tap the information base.

The executive has to acquire an ability to exploit analogies, employ criteria, assess information, discover sources of information, and come to know pertinent qualitative and quantitative analytical techniques. Executives must have at their command specific skills such as mathematics (especially arithmetic), common sense, statistics, analysis, and priority setting.

Mathematics arranges and manipulates data; arithmetic studies the various uses of numbers. Common sense relates to the use of practical and ordinary intelligence, and at times it can be used instead of more rigorous analysis. One should use caution in always relying on common sense. Statistics is a measurement based on mathematical probability provides and often is calculated from a sample of an entire situation (a model). Statistical information can have important economic, political, and social implications. To help executives make decisions, analysts break problems into constituent parts to gain insight into their nature, their properties, and how they relate to one another. As to priority setting, decisionmakers have no more important skills than those associated with setting precedence in time, order, importance, or other factors. They have to know where to focus attention. Above all, they have to be able to determine what weights to assign to the various components of a problem.

Effective decisionmakers have to be minimally aware of what these qualitative and quantitative techniques are, especially the tools of arithmetic and statistics. At times executives overlook pertinent facts when making decisions and can apply hindsight to gain a truer picture of a resulting situation.

PART II

Alternate Outcomes

CHAPTER 9

Problem Substitution

To avoid operating in disappointing situations, executives apply solutions. They set up a series of benchmarks to determine the extent to which these solutions have eradicated problems. This chapter assesses this traditional approach to problems and suggests a more effective alternative.

ESTABLISHING OBJECTIVES

Chapter 2 briefly discussed the subject of setting objectives. In this chapter it is important to note that in assessing the impact of solutions executives tend to establish such objectives and then evaluate how their remedies affect these goals. Peter Drucker (1969, p. 306) notes what logic should tell any competent executive, namely, that "[o]bjectives are needed in every area where performance and results directly and vitally affect the survival and prosperity of the business." Drucker lists a number of areas in which organizations might assign objectives: market standing, innovation, productivity, physical and financial resources, profitability, manager performance and development, performance of workers, and public responsibility. Bruce Baird (1978, pp. 9–11) also argues that individuals must have a goal in mind before they can recognize that a problem exists. In viewing problems, effective executives are called on to be "proactive." They should want to "fix" the problem in order to attain a beneficial objective (Plunkett and Hale, 1982, p. 60).

Yet by slavishly depending on an "objectives" approach, executives can produce ironic results. In trying to meet one of these ends, they can harm others. Traditionally the nation seeks the goal of achieving a strong economy. However, if it begins to attain the objective of a "booming" economy, instead of rejoicing, economists often begin to fear inflation. In such cases, the Federal Reserve Bank might increase discount rates, drying up money and slowing down the economy. It aims to avoid increased unemployment or depressed incomes. Because of such probable outcomes, decisionmakers should carefully think through probable consequences before relying totally on an "objectives" prism through which to determine success or failure.

COMPONENT PROBLEMS

In addition to the preceding caution, executives should take care because rarely does a problem exist in isolation. More often it comprises several parts, called "component problems" in this study. For example, the CEO of a well-known breakfast food company became very disappointed in recent sales. During his investigations, he tried to determine any changes that he should make in the firm's operating objectives. He then asked a series of pertinent questions: Does the firm's cereal become too soggy in milk? Do the flakes really taste like cardboard, as critics suggest? Does the cereal contain enough nutrients? Has the firm's advertising appeal become unpopular? Do store owners display the product on inconspicuous shelves, causing people to miss it? Is the firm charging too high an introductory price? As one can see, the sales problem had several component parts.

One also must consider the extent to which the component problems are susceptible to quantitative measurement. As a rule, executives find it harder to attach meaningful numbers to social phenomena than to physical traits. They find it easier to discover how many pineapples field-workers harvest in a specified time than how happy these same workers are during the same work period. Of course, analysts can use polls to help grind out "truth" from messy, cluttered, unstable situations. In some instances these "data devices" in themselves become politically controversial and emotional.

PERMANENCE OF PROBLEMS

When contemplating the use of objectives, executives should consider not only that problems comprise component problems but that these components often last a long time. It is well here to reiterate the obvious fact that human beings always live with problems. No historical era has enjoyed, nor will any ever enjoy, a problem-free existence. (See Chapter 11 for a discussion of utopias.) Even people living during "golden ages" contended with unhappy times. When Homer spoke of the Golden Age in Aegean Minoan culture, he depicted a civilization better than his own. The sixteenth and seventeenth centuries B.C. are regarded as the zenith of Aegean civilization, the Golden Age of Crete (Durant, 1954a, p. 8). Yet even in Homer's day Crete's strength was beginning to decay. The island began to lose its forests, perhaps population control went too far, lust for physical pleasure sapped the vitality of the race, and the people began to lose the will to defend themselves. These same dynamics of rise and decline are present today.

After World War II, the United States was stronger economically than any other nation on earth but began to lose steam. The United States gained economic preeminence in the 1950s, largely because (1) in the preceding 80 years it maintained a higher rate of productivity than other nations and (2) other nations suffered horrendous physical and manpower losses during World War II. This country's relative position declined in the latter half of the twentieth century because of a slip in productivity.

Likewise, the executives who led Xerox in its early days of rapid growth eventually had to come to grips with a company losing steam and facing an increase in the number and gravity of problems. The company found itself confronting major problems, such as finding enough investment capital, designing an effective organization, hiring well-qualified professionals, and just as important, keeping qualified employees with the firm.

At first glance, to state that executives always face problems seems a bromide. When people forget that they always confront some troubles, they invite unpleasant surprise. Nonetheless, this trite remark does merit attention. Placing it as one of the centerpieces in this work seems well justified. Readers would do well to think about this abiding "reality" when altering old, or charting new, directions.

ERADICATING PROBLEMS

Although problems persist, not *all* problems endure. Certainly, over the years, executives have cleaned up many messes. In most Western countries slave labor, deplorable wages, sweatshops, child labor, and unsafe and filthy factories have just about disappeared. In the twentieth century, people can be proud of the many disagreeable situations that they have remedied and that they most likely will continue to ameliorate in the coming century.

In moments of unbounded exuberance, executives seem to think in terms of eliminating problems altogether. One finds books with exciting titles like *The Complete Problem Solver: A Total System for Competitive Decision Making* (Arnold, 1992). Such a label conveys the image of a bulldozer solution preparing to smash through barricades of ignorance on the way to achieving "total victory" or "complete enlightenment." Conversely, one looks in vain for phrases like *"partial* problem solving," "solving *some key features* of problems," or "solving *some components* of problems." Whether they state so explicitly, all too many bosses seem to want the 100 percent solution.

Perfectly down-to-earth, highly placed public officials, at times, seem to ask for total removal of a grand national ill. In 1996 President Bill Clinton called on the states to enact a "zero tolerance" policy against people under 21 years of age who drink and drive. In 1993 alcohol played a major part in more than 17,000 (or 43.5 percent of all) fatal accidents. Some 2,200 people died in automobile crashes attributed to young drunk drivers. Yet critics might contend that the president should have known better than to expect the states to prosecute *all* adult drunk drivers. Although everyone knows that the states will fail to prosecute all violators, the president perhaps believed that by advocating such a complete goal the nation stood a better chance of making at least some progress ("Drugs and Alcohol," 1997).

Figure 9.1 illustrates this less-than-adequate way of addressing problems. As illustrated in this graph, decisionmakers have become transfixed with the principle that attaining a 100 percent solution constitutes the natural, indeed the only correct, way of addressing problems. In this example, they proceed through a series of milestones, years 1980 to 2000 (along the horizontal axis). In the process, executives aim to gain constantly a larger percentage of total predetermined goals (along the right vertical axis). The two hypothetical trend lines in this graph demonstrate an executive's performance. Trend A is disappointing. Here executives achieve only a little over half of their five predetermined objectives. Trend B shows success by the year 2000, as they seem to have attained all the objectives. Yet this approach has a number of flaws. For example, as we have stated, decisionmakers cannot always have full confidence that they have correctly identified all the goals that they desire and need.

Above all, the most flagrant error of executives in this case results from their failure to consider the new problems that they create as they seek to solve old ones. Figure 9.1 suffers because throughout its course it displays only a fraction of the problems that existed at the time that decisionmakers implemented solutions. In Figure 9.2 the years 1980 to 1995 represent the milestones. During this period, new problems emerge. The important point to remember is that not all, but some, of these new problems result from attempts to solve the original problems. When this happens, any judgment about the effectiveness of a solution must take into account the new problems that remedies generate.

Thus, while in Trend B executives might believe that they have ended up solving all their problems, in reality they still suffer from new problems that do not show up in the curve. They might have achieved only 80 or

Figure 9.1
Focus on Achieving Objectives

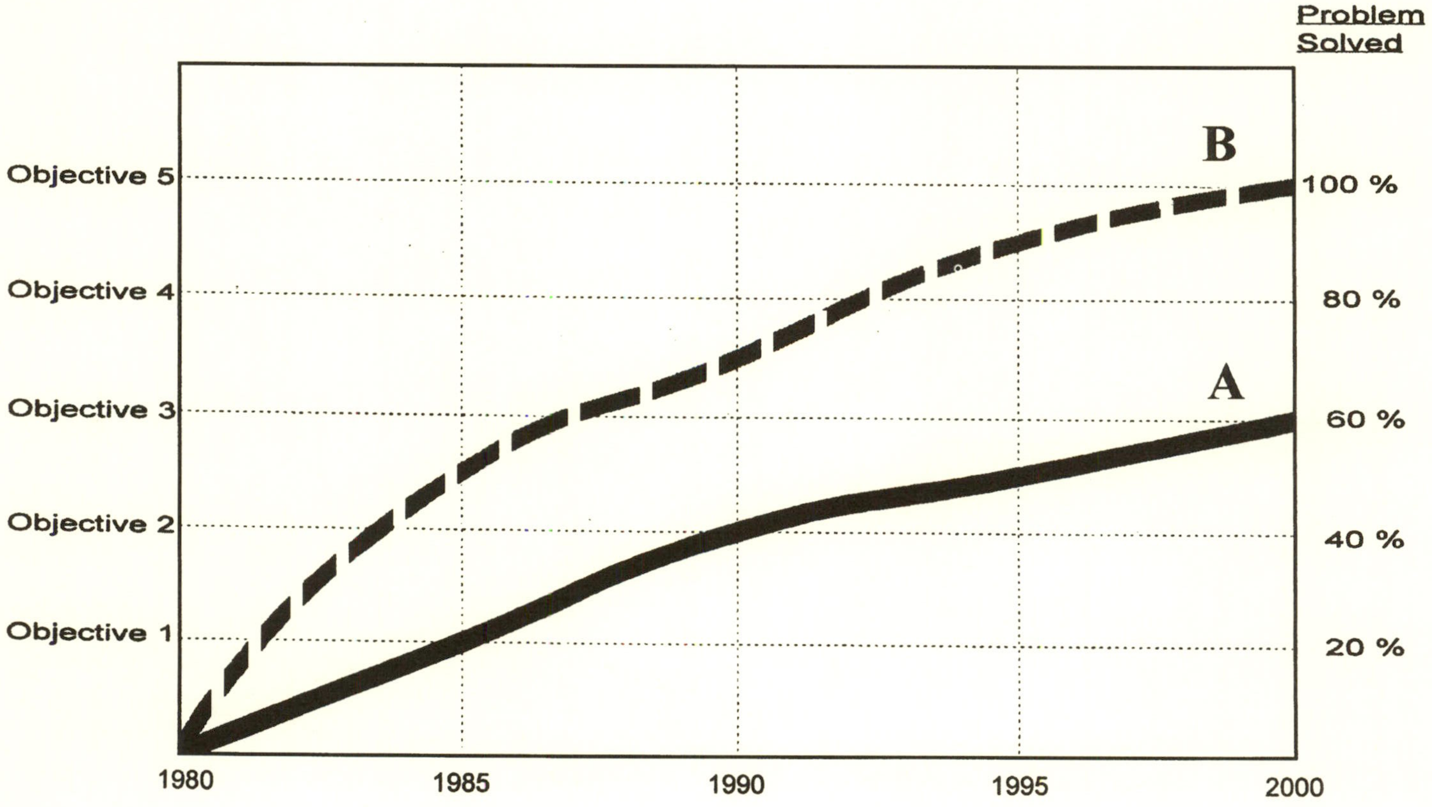

Figure 9.2
Problem Exchange Ratio (Hypothetical Ratios)

Solved Problems/Total Problems					
Situation	1980	1985	1990	1995	Ratio of Solved to Total Problems
1	0/25	5/25	10/25	20/25	80 percent
2	0/30	5/30	5/30	25/30	83 percent
3	0/15	4/17	9/24	12/24	50 percent
4	0/20	15/20	15/35	15/45	33 percent
5	0/15	5/15	6/15	6/15	40 percent

60 percent of the *new* total, giving them a completely different and unfavorable status.

One more point on this subject deserves mention. In getting rid of unwanted conditions, executives should understand the need for periodic assessments. By and large, they cannot eliminate all troubles in one grand swoop. It simply takes time to jettison distasteful situations and to adjust to new, improved ones.

THE PROBLEM EXCHANGE RATIO

We come to a key concept suggested by this work—the problem exchange ratio (PER). The PER is the ratio of problems solved to the total number of problems remaining after executives have applied solutions. As shown in Figure 9.2, analysts can measure performance over a number of years, from 1980 to 1995 in this case. They can measure the status of a situation at each year. By using the PER, they can calculate if things are going well, going badly, or remaining the same.

Decisionmakers have to take actions in order to overcome problems. They then judge their performance in terms of successes or failures. If executives can identify the totality of problems, theoretically they stand the best chance of doing away with unsatisfactory conditions. Yet individuals seldom accomplish identification fully.

Executives can only measure the effectiveness of their performance imprecisely (at least until researchers develop more and better ways to analyze the dynamics of problems). To reemphasize a central point of this work, they can do this by assessing the probable success or failure of their actions vis-à-vis the component problems that confront them over time (Hickman and Silva, 1984, pp. 21–25).

The PER rests on the notion that when decisionmakers apply solutions, they theoretically can produce three inevitable effects. First, they can remedy all component problems that face them—in effect, eliminating all unsatisfactory conditions. Second, they can cure some components, but not all, leaving behind some problems requiring additional remedies. Figure 9.1 illustrates these effects. Third, by their very nature, solutions generate new, unanticipated problems of their own. As Donald Gause and Gerald Weinberg (1982, p. 533) have said: "Each solution is the source of the next problem." This effect appears in Figure 9.2. Executives seem to pay less attention to the third effect.

By applying PER, they replace one set of problems with another, hoping in the process to come out ahead. Specifically, they attempt to judge the worth of a solution by balancing the problems that they have solved to the total problems remaining, including new ones that they still have to solve. The higher the ratio of component problems solved to total problems remaining, the more executives come out ahead.

Periodic Identification

How does one go about determining progress or slippages in performance at different times? First, the researcher assesses the situation at the outset and then periodically contrasts the status between milestones during the decisionmaking period. Figure 9.2 illustrates a hypothetical series of PER procedures during the period under examination. In the first situation executives initially face 25 unsolved component problems. Although the same 25 component problems remain during the entire period under review, executives solve 20 problems (or 80 percent) of the total by 1995, indicating great success.

Situation 2 tells a somewhat more successful story. Faced initially with 30 unsolved problems, decisionmakers solve only 5 by 1985 and retain that number to 1990. Then, with a seemingly strong burst of creativity, executives solve 20 more component problems by 1995, ending with 25 solved problems (83 percent of total problems solved).

Situation 3 tells a more complex story. At the beginning executives face 15 unsolved component problems. By 1985 they solve 4 of these, but as they apply their solutions, they introduce an additional 2 component problems, leaving a total of 17 problems (of which 13 remain unsolved). By 1990 executives solve 5 more component problems, but solutions add 7 component problems, leaving a total of 9 out of the 24 solved. By 1995 they correct 3 more component problems and create no new ones, leaving a final problem exchange ratio of 50 percent of total problems solved. This ratio compares favorably with some 24 percent achieved in 1985.

Let's contrast this accounting of the success of solutions to the illustration in Figure 9.1. Suppose that the 12 component problems eventually solved were among the 15 present in 1980. A careless executive might conclude that 12 out of 15 component problems (80 percent) had been solved when in fact the solution was much less successful because of the new problems generated. Saying that the solution solved 50 percent of problems of the total at hand is a much more accurate reflection of the real success of the solutions implemented.

In Situation 4 executives initially face 20 unsolved component problems. They initially experience great progress, solving 15 of the 20 by 1985. However, by 1990 conditions worsen. The solutions that they try create 15 more component problems by 1990 and 10 additional ones by 1995. Consequently, they solve one-third of total component problems at the end of the period, probably a disappointing ratio.

Finally, Situation 5 shows executives starting out with an unsatisfactory status of 15 component problems and ending up with the same number. Their solutions added no more component problems. By 1985 analysts solve 5 component problems and 1 more by 1990, maintaining 6 to 1995. At the end of the period, executives have a ratio of 40 percent of solved to total component problems.

The history of various industries, programs, or projects reflects the situations illustrated in Figure 9.2. Situations 1 and 2 show steady progress with little or no additional problems later in the period. History records that the polio vaccine took some 20 years to diffuse but engendered few additional component problems during its lifetime. Situation 3 also shows steady progress in solving component problems early in the time period. However, increasingly solutions generate new problems. In the early years the automobile industry solved most of its original problems, but as millions took to the road, a host of new problems emerged. Society had to contend with serious pollution, additional and more serious safety deficiencies, traffic jams, and the like.

At first, Situation 4 demonstrates dramatic progress. Executives solve 15 of the original 20 component problems by 1985. However, later it suffers from many new component problems. The nuclear power industry demonstrates this trend. In the early decades after World War II several nations built nuclear power plants relatively quickly. For example, the French constructed their first nuclear power plant in 1957 and by 1978 built 54 more.

Researchers had solved the major problems of converting fission technology into usable electric power. However, in later years the nuclear power industry came to face some tough component problems that resisted solution. The long-term storage of radioactive wastes and fuels, the skyrocketing costs of building new nuclear power plants, the question of insurance against major accidents, and other thorny difficulties arose to plague the nuclear power industry. As a result of these burgeoning problems, the United States, at the present time, is not building or planning to build any new nuclear power plants.

In Situation 5, modest rather than dramatic progress takes place throughout the period. Such progress is noted with new medicines when the side effects limit success (e.g., the use of cortisone to relieve inflammation).

A Question of Weighting

It also should be pointed out that all the component problems in this example carry equal weight. Such a situation rarely exists in real life. Thus, executives actually might confront a more difficult analytical problem than appears in Figure 9.2. To derive an exact PER, they probably would give more weight or less weight to various component problems. For example, in Situation 4, the 15 additional component problems appearing in 1990 could be 20 times more difficult than the weight of the original component problems. Under these circumstances the final ratio of solved to total problems might prove much poorer than the 33 percent shown in Figure 9.2. Conversely, the new problems might be of less weight, producing a better ratio.

Executives would have to address these component problems as they do the problems appearing in Figure 8.1. Using subjective judgments, they would have to rank the seriousness of problems and then calculate the PER. Obviously, the calculations would become more complicated.

Practical Assessment

At this point it pays to mention briefly some specific criteria that executives might examine in evaluating PERs. Above all, they have to determine the validity of the PER. How much confidence do they have in its usefulness? Naturally, decisionmakers prefer that PERs do what they want them to do. Just as important, decisionmakers are concerned with the relevance of PERs. Are PERs pertinent and appropriate to the matter at hand and are they useful to decisionmakers? Will the methods associated with PERs prove effective in assessing the relative gravity of problems? By telling executives where they stand, the PER models should give executives the necessary insight to change a situation for the better. These executives would welcome this assistance.

Executives also are concerned whether PERs tell them something beyond what is apparent from direct observation (without using PERs). Obviously, if executives can come to understand the relative gravity of problems without applying a PER, then why resort to it? PERs should tell decisionmakers something new and important. They should provide executives with more effective tools to get their jobs done. It avails executives little if they apply well-known solutions that cannot overcome new types of problems.

Even if individuals become satisfied with the significance of PERs, they also have to judge the efficiency of the approach. Have they applied too many resources to gain the insights that they need in judging the status of problems? Business and public service institutions can obtain less than optimal results for the amount of resources that they invest in assessing problems. Lastly, in using PERs, executives must seek timeliness in ascertaining what they confront. Will the information appear in time to meet the decision points of executives, becoming available before a situation deteriorates beyond redemption?

PER Sagas

Three major situations are illustrated in Figure 9.3. Column A contains cases in which executives have either entirely or largely solved component problems. Under Column B are found episodes in which component problems have been partially solved. Column C lists instances in which researchers added (new) component problems as they attempted to solve existing ones.

Smallpox Saga (Column A)

The smallpox case illustrates an episode in which researchers and health administrators totally eradicated a serious problem (Joshua Schwartz, 1979, pp. 181–193). Throughout much of history, smallpox was a dreaded scourge. Smallpox, an infectious disease caused by a virus, affects the patient with a fever, followed by an eruption of pustules that eventually leave scars. Victims catch the disease through direct and indirect contact with the virus. The disease caused an estimated 2 million deaths worldwide in 1967. Applying large-scale vaccinations, especially of children before their first birthday, virtually has eliminated this affliction. In 1977, the World Health Organization (WHO), an agency of the United Nations, undertook a huge project to eradicate smallpox worldwide. In addition to vaccinating millions, WHO employed and trained large numbers of medical professionals and used modern communications, transportation, information, medical facilities, and medical equipment.

Between 1977 and 1980, only a handful of cases were reported throughout the world. The virtual eradication of smallpox represents one of the most successful efforts to solve a major problem completely.

IBM 360 Computer (Column A)

In the twentieth century, International Business Machines emerged as the major computer manufacturer (Watson, 1963). People soon learned

Figure 9.3
Cases Illustrating Problem Inquiry

Column A	Column B	Column C
Solved Entire Problem	*Solved Some of Problem/ Components*	*Added Problems/ Components*
• Smallpox Case • 360 Computer Case	• War on Cancer Case • Xerox Case	• Green Revolution Case • Chamberlain Case

that the computer, a machine for processing and calculating data, acquired, recorded, stored, analyzed, and distributed huge amounts of information. In recent years, the computer probably contributed more to changing how private firms and public agencies make decisions than any other single executive tool. By the mid-1960s, the device already had exerted extraordinary influence. Until the personal computer (miniprocessor) appeared in the 1970s, IBM designers concentrated on building mainframe computers.

These large, stationary, and centralized mainframe computers had a prodigious memory and an enormous ability to perform mathematical functions instantaneously. The case that follows discusses IBM's decision to move to a large, dramatically improved 360 mainframe computer (Bradley, 1990).

Early IBM History. IBM was incorporated in 1911. Under Thomas Watson, the firm assembled a highly motivated, well-trained, and well-paid staff. In its early years the company experienced considerable growth. Watson put IBM on the map (Watson, 1990, p. viii).

The business climate of the 1920s seemed ideally suited for developing an office equipment industry. During this period, IBM flourished chiefly in the sales and leasing of office machines. After 1929, the Great Depression affected the office machine business. In its efforts to overcome the Depression, the American public turned to new political and governmental intervention. Franklin Roosevelt's New Deal offered specific programs designed to revive the economy and to relieve troubled social conditions. Firms found that they had to process ever-increasing amounts of information, much of it demanded by public agencies (Sobel, 1981, p. 71). Business machines offered a way of gaining more effective direction of that information. Federal agencies turned to this equipment in administering their many new programs.

U.S. industry prospered during World War II (Milward, 1979, p. 51). So did the computer industry. The war vastly increased the demand for information, and IBM worked to meet this demand. After World War II, the company continued to prosper, but by the 1960s its executives saw some major troubles ahead. Through the years, IBM faced a series of risky economic choices. Peter Drucker has pointed out that in seeking to strike out in new directions effective entrepreneurs use systematic reasoning to lessen the severity of risk. In confronting the challenge of the computer industry, IBM conformed to Drucker's observation (Drucker, 1985, pp. 28–29, 52–56). The company knew that it would have to make risky large investments if it wanted to develop new machines. It continued to conduct expensive research and development.

Targeting the Key Problem. In the early 1960s, IBM's executives concluded that with the technology and corporate strength available the firm would not be able to meet anticipated demand. In time, a less-than-adequate capacity began causing serious problems. The firm defined one of its basic problems as runaway demand for information. IBM's executives also were concerned that the firm could not raise from its own internal sources the huge amounts of capital required to develop and market a highly advanced 360 mainframe computer.

This instrument represented IBM's answer to the need for a compatible family of computers—pieces of equipment that could "talk" among themselves. The firm first studied the market very carefully, estimating what the future might hold. Its decisionmakers then concluded that the 360 mainframe could become a commercial winner. However, IBM could count on success only if it achieved a breakthrough in a new technology—the integrated circuit. Thomas Watson, Jr. picked T.V. Learson, a company vice president, as the project leader (Learson, 1968).

To finance a new generation of machines, IBM borrowed heavily. In fact, some people came to think of IBM as a bank with manufacturing subsidiaries. The corporation made more money from leasing its equipment than from selling it outright. Fortunately, IBM enjoyed a highly liquid situation. When the company began the 360 program, it took advantage of its excellent financial position and, for the most part, spent its money wisely. Because the computer industry was undergoing rapid technological change, it presented a high risk. In fact, another official referred to the project as "You Bet Your Company" (a play of words on a popular television quiz show of the period) (Twiss, 1974, p. 22; Wise, 1966). Moreover, IBM executives knew that if the company developed a new computer, its second-generation equipment would become obsolete as soon as its third generation, the 360, came on line.

IBM took a $5 billion gamble because the potential gain seemed so enormous. Instead of costing $1.38 per computation, the 360 had an estimated cost of $0.035 per computation. IBM was confident that its talented and trained people could do the job. The critical point here is that IBM's leaders identified the correct problems impeding their efforts to strengthen the financial health and future of the company. Above all, IBM's leadership recognized that it had chosen the best individual as the project leader. Learson enjoyed the respect of his people. They believed that he asked the right questions and was not afraid of making hard decisions. For example, he had IBM scrap all projects that competed with the 360. Despite inevitable internal squabbles and external pressures, on April 7, 1964, the company announced that it was taking the 360 plunge.

Rewards of Success. After pouring huge resources into 360 development, IBM found that it had solved many of the toughest problems affecting its future. Success ensured IBM's continued near-monopoly of the data-processing machine industry throughout the world. The success of IBM, in part, forced major competitors, such as the Radio Corporation of America (RCA) and the General Electric Company, to withdraw from the competition. IBM built six large new plants in France, Germany, and the United States. In five years, the company expanded its workforce by more than 50,000 employees worldwide, increasing its payroll by a third.

In evaluating the 360 episode, Robert Sobel suggested that the great gamble paid off—and in ways that could not have been anticipated. IBM had in mind a family of technologically advanced computers that would give it the undisputed lead in technology, expand its markets, ward off competitors, and unite the company. The firm succeeded in meeting these goals (Sobel, 1981, p. 232). In terms of its immediate situation, IBM totally solved its most important problems. Thus, in this work we placed the 360 computer episode in the first category.

Pitfalls of Success. By developing the 360 computer, IBM solved almost all of its major problems, but only for a certain period of time. No organization gets rid of all unwanted conditions forever. After a while IBM found itself with new problems, some that it had not anticipated. First, given its undisputed leadership in the field, IBM faced a host of troublesome antitrust actions (Bradley, 1990). Thus, the new computer created temporary problems of increasing demand for money. Perhaps the most serious problem of all, by continuing to allocate most resources to maintaining its leadership in the mainframe field, IBM ignored the small-sized personal computer business. These minicomputers captured an increasingly large share of the future market, and other companies became strong competitors in the ensuing years (Peters, 1992, pp. 487–488).

However, by the latter half of the 1990s IBM had recovered to a remarkable extent because, as its CEO suggested, "We are completely transforming the business to address the market for networked computer systems" (Mills, 1996, p. 78).

War on Cancer (Column B)

People fear cancer perhaps more than any other disease. Not only do they panic at the thought of certain death from some types of cancer, but they dread the pain that sometimes accompanies the disease and the treatments that make them sick. Because the medical profession now has more effective drugs available and has improved drug and radiation therapy, the number of deaths caused by cancer for patients under 30 years of age is decreasing. Moreover, doctors can cure most patients suffering from certain specific cancers diagnosed in the early stages. Even patients with advanced cases of some cancers have a chance of cure.

On the other hand, the number of deaths from cancer is increasing in the population as a whole. This increase in deaths exists despite the fact that a little less than 30 years ago in his State of the Union message President Richard M. Nixon declared "war on cancer" and committed an additional initial $100 million to the National Cancer Plan (Burger, p. 41, 1980). Researchers have had almost three decades to lick the problem. On the positive side, they have made significant progress with the additional resources that the federal government has allocated during this time period.

In major respects, however, the war has faltered. It certainly has not been as successful as the fight against smallpox. Because cancer originates in a variety of complex forms, many calling for different therapies, researchers have found it hard to gain the knowledge they need to develop effective treatment. For example, physicians have failed to find a chemotherapeutic treatment that under all instances would kill all malignant tumor cells without also destroying neighboring healthy tissue.

The important point for this discussion is that the war against cancer has solved some of the component problems associated with this dread disease but has failed to solve others. Enough unanswered questions remain that the thought of having cancer still triggers great fear.

Xerox Case (Column B)

It is well to reiterate that even successful companies, exploiting the most advanced technologies, cannot get rid of all (or sometimes even most) problems. The story of the Xerox company supports this conclusion. Beginning as a pygmy venture, the Xerox company no doubt identified many of the right components of its problems and found effective ways to respond to them. As a photocopy business, Xerox grew into a giant corporation (Jacobson and Hillkirk, 1987). Xerox continues to expend enormous resources to continue research (e.g., lowering the unit price, improving the quality of its reproductions, adding color).

In the meantime, Xerox searched for and devised new uses for its photocopying machines. One should remember that from its origins Xerox made tremendous advances in reducing the size of the machine from one that required a fairly large, air-conditioned room to a small desktop unit. Yet after its explosive early growth, Xerox has not remedied certain problems.

To achieve proper production and distribution, the company had, among other chores, to train skilled and efficient workforces and constantly update training. It had to ensure adequate quality control, design an effective advertising campaign, perform critical marketing tasks, procure and maintain fleets of vehicles to transport products, prepare and distribute ancillary equipment, and fashion proper accounting practices. Given the increasingly competitive market in which it operated, especially with the entry of foreign manufacturers, Xerox searched for problems that arose as the environment changed. Its leaders sought to solve these problems with the objective of starting new, profitable business ventures. It took great delight in successfully repelling the aggressive Japanese assault on its core business in the world market (Moskowitz, Levering, and Katz, 1990, pp. 419–421).

Xerox's executives did this by recognizing that customers change their needs and habits and demand products of highest quality. The firm examined the problem of quality control very carefully and, by 1982, some 92 percent of the parts that Xerox shipped were defect free; by 1988, Xerox's parts were more than 99 percent defect free. Xerox won the Baldridge National Quality Award in 1989 for its achievement in this field (Moskowitz, Levering, and Katz, 1990, pp. 419–421). The company continued to maintain a lean labor force and took extra efforts to train its people and to give them favorable working conditions. The firm still enjoyed relatively good relations with its employees, despite being forced to reduce the size of its workforce (Lydenberg et al., 1986, pp. 37–38).

Even in these efforts the firm made some mistakes. Like IBM, it failed to identify the opportunities associated with personal computers. Although Xerox did identify the need for personal computer equipment and the connection between its technology and the computer and did do some initial development, its Palo Alto Research Center (PARC) failed to develop the hardware to the point of commercial exploitation.

The new Apple company picked up many of the ideas that PARC spawned and went on to become an early leader in the field of personal computers. It showed great interest in overcoming the gross dissatisfaction that owners felt in operating the small computers then on the market. As is well known, Apple designed "user-friendly" computers. That is, Apple computers were easy to operate. By moving headlong into the small-computer field, this small, high-risk company matured into a mammoth firm in the field, surpassing Xerox.

However, Xerox executives did not become immobilized. The industry did not find them totally asleep at the switch when new opportunities began to present themselves. They early on discerned the growing problem of financial services within the American market. Thus, by the 1980s, copiers represented less than half of Xerox sales. The company established Xerox credit and added a property casualty insurer and two investment banking firms (Moskowitz, Levering, and Katz, 1990, pp. 419–421). As Xerox changed its emphasis, it had to explore very closely the problems in the credit market that it might convert to business opportunities. In the

1990s, Xerox faced other difficulties and had to make reductions in its workforce.

Green Revolution (Column C)

The Green Revolution has been a definite boon to the world's hungry (Basiuk, 1977, pp. 141–143, 187; Sardar and Rosser-Owen, 1977, pp. 535–575). However, as it solved some of the problems of rural less-developed regions of the world, it triggered new major component problems. In the late 1960s, the Green Revolution enabled farmers in underdeveloped countries, especially India, Pakistan, and the Philippines, to boost farm production considerably. Agronomists, notably Nobel Prize winner Norman E. Borlaug, cultivated high-yielding, disease-resistant, and nutritious varieties of hybrid strains of wheat, rice, and maize. Research institutions like the Rockefeller Foundation and the Ford Foundation made important contributions to the development of high-yielding strains of cereal grains (Myrdal, 1981, pp. 215–225). Countries that had been net importers of foodstuffs became net exporters or at least became self-sufficient. These were large achievements.

Why did the Green Revolution, hailed as a major breakthrough in food production, turn out to be a mixed blessing? The answer lies in the fact that these new crops became more vulnerable to pest epidemics and climatic fluctuations. The chances of unfavorable conditions causing very high and widespread losses arose, a consequence less likely with formerly diversified, low-yield, local variety crops. As indicated, the new kind of farming depended on relatively uniform varieties of crops.

Of greater importance, however, the new varieties demanded more energy, more fertilizer, and more water, all expensive items (Revelle, 1981, pp. 142–143). These technologies demanded that farmers raise what to them seemed like large amounts of money. Joining the money economy greatly changed their lives. They had never before faced these novel component problems in any major way. In addition, the need for more capital forced poor peasants off the land, leading to a concentration of land ownership by the rich and greedy.

Furthermore, to make improved farming a reality, peasants had to transform their societies and change how they farmed (Rao, 1973, pp. 451–452) and lived. To be effective, technology diffusion entails two-way communications—informing farmers (particularly those of low income) about the results of research and telling researchers what farmers want and need. The Consultative Group on International Agricultural Research (CGIAR), for example, supports a network of international research centers, which have earned a reputation for developing and distributing modern farm technologies throughout the world.

Although the Green Revolution was very successful and improved the overall agricultural situation in developing countries, it brought about new troubles and did not end malnutrition and famine worldwide, especially in those regions plagued by brutal and bloody internecine tribal conflicts (Granger, 1979, p. 105; Sanders, 1983, pp. 171, 292).

Chamberlain Case (Column C)

Figure 9.3 also contains cases in which officials made matters worse by adding new and vexing problems. Perhaps no individual added more problems of greater gravity and seriousness to those already facing his nation than did Great Britain's Prime Minister Neville Chamberlain in 1938. In modern history, no event proved more inimical and damaging to a nation's self-interest than the Munich debacle of 1938. It made World War II inevitable (Morgenthau and Thompson, 1985, p. 6).

Just before World War II, Chamberlain seemed to believe that England's greatest problem was *preventing* a major war from erupting in Europe. He seemed to fear that England inevitably would be caught up in this unwanted conflict. In reality, England's most critical problem related to *stopping Hitler* from achieving his aggressive designs in Europe and elsewhere (even if England had to go to war to do it).

Yet because he failed to recognize his chief problem, when meeting Hitler in Munich in 1938, Chamberlain caved in to Hitler's demand for German occupation of the Sudentenland (with its German population) of Czechoslovakia (Palmer and Colton, 1984, pp. 801–804). He displayed an appeasement so stark and craven that afterwards people likened any act of caving in to aggression as the "Munich" syndrome. From the tarmac at the London airport, Chamberlain vigorously waved a piece of paper over his head, shouting that this agreement with Hitler meant "peace with honor, I believe that it is peace in our time." Five months later, Hitler totally ignored the Munich agreement and took over the rest of Czechoslovakia. About a year afterward, World War II erupted with the Nazi invasion of Poland.

Because the British had not prepared for war, Chamberlain had little alternative but appeasement. In large measure, Britain's lack of preparation resulted from a conscious policy by Chamberlain not to increase defense production. Winston Churchill had bombarded the Chamberlain government with demands to reorganize and develop a ministry of supply (Churchill, 1948, p. 212). Chamberlain repeatedly rejected Churchill's advice, fearing that to begin rearming would prompt Hitler to launch aggressive actions. What a tragic reading of history!

In large part, this reluctance explains why Britain found itself so militarily weak on the eve of World War II. Chamberlain could not follow more robust policies against Hitler because England had little with which to back them up. Instead, he had to assure Hitler of Britain's peaceful intentions (Churchill, 1948, p. 212). However, if Chamberlain had not held his mistaken belief about Hitler, he probably would have accelerated arms production earlier, and the world might have been spared one of the most destructive periods in history.

SUMMARY

In overcoming problems, executives tend to set goals and then assess how their corrections influence these ends. These objectives relate to the problems that executives confront. Problems rarely appear as single entities. Rather, they tend to be composed of component problems. Executives often think that they have to get rid of a problem or suffer it. Although some problems persist, others do not endure, as illustrated in the economic and social history of Western civilization.

Figure 9.1 illustrates an inadequate way to view the task of addressing the effectiveness of solutions. Executives set the objectives that they have to attain to eradicate the problems facing them and then proceed to achieve them over time. In this instance, executives do not consider the problems that they create as they apply solutions.

The key idea in this chapter is the problem exchange ratio (PER). The PER is the ratio of problems solved to the total number of problems remaining after remedies have been tried. The PER indicates that decisionmakers either come out ahead or behind in terms of whether they increase or decrease the percentage of problems solved to total problems remaining. Figure 9.2 illustrates this more accurate PER method, which takes into account the new problems created when decisionmakers apply solutions.

Situations 1 and 2 resemble the polio vaccine, which experienced major initial progress and later hardly any (as few advances were really needed later). Situation 3 is like the automobile industry, which showed early promise in overcoming problems; but as people used the automobile more and more, new problems were generated. Situation 4 reflects the nuclear power industry, which solved its early problems but later suffered many new ones. Situation 5 illustrates the use of cortisone injected into inflamed joints to relieve arthritis. Modest progress takes place throughout the period of this medicine's use.

The chapter discussed cases that illustrated specific PERs. In the smallpox and IBM 360 cases, the PERs came out way ahead; in the case of smallpox the problem was entirely eliminated. In the War on Cancer and Xerox cases, executives solved many of the key component problems but still confronted others that resisted solution. In the Green Revolution and Chamberlain cases, executives created new component problems as they tried to solve existing ones. In the Chamberlain episode, these new problems proved disastrous.

CHAPTER 10

Degrees of Effectiveness

By bringing about desired consequences, executives try to come to terms with or to outlast their problems. The rise of American industry to a predominant position in the world after World War II resulted from the efforts of entrepreneurs to solve problems standing in the way of improved productivity and efficiency (Barber, 1962, p. 211). To a considerable degree, these entrepreneurs targeted real problems and applied analytical methods that brought the essence of the problem to light, enabling executives to move ahead in achieving their objectives.

However, executives cannot always determine precisely the outcomes that result from decisions (Alden, 1997). A number of difficulties interfere with evaluating the effects of solutions. Executives have few exact measures with which to make such evaluations, and thus results frequently remain open to interpretation. Naturally, interpretations have a tendency to differ. In addition, at times major decisions have few immediate outcomes, as conditions and the interests of executives change. Often individual executives have only limited control, as extraneous factors mask results and obscure causal relationships. Finally, decisionmakers might implement only one alternative (i.e., the recommendation), and they never know what would have happened on "the road not taken."

Yet the fact remains that institutions still have to adjust to the changes brought about by solutions, and decisionmakers have to come to understand the changes associated with those outcomes. As unwanted conditions

Figure 10.1
Cases Illustrating Problem-Solving Effectiveness

Column A	Column B	Column C
Solved Entirely	*Coping*	*Accommodating*
•GI Bill Case •Thalidomide Case	•Job's Case •MCI Case	•Belize Case •Blow-Mold Packers Case

disappear, executives have to design new strategies to address the new problems that emerge (Jun and Storm, 1973, pp. 296–309).

Figure 10.1 presents the titles of cases in which executives have addressed problems. In some instances they gained a favorable outcome or at least avoided unfavorable consequences. In others they still had to live with unwanted circumstances. First, in the GI Bill and thalidomide cases (as in the smallpox and 360 computer cases in Chapter 9), it can be argued that executives cured their problems totally. Second, in the cases of Job and MCI, those in charge did not passively accept the unwanted or distasteful lot given them but worked to change it by fierce argumentation and other efforts. Third, in the Belize and Blow-Mold Packers cases, decisionmakers accepted unhappy situations in the hope that conditions would not get worse.

SOLVED ENTIRELY

GI Bill Case (Column A)

At the end of World War II, the United States faced a huge problem when millions of veterans suddenly flooded the labor market. These generally undereducated ex-servicemen and -women lacked the new knowledge demanded in the postwar period. U.S. political leaders anticipated that major economic dislocations would result and passed the Servicemen's Readjustment Act of 1944, otherwise known as the GI Bill (Hathorn, Penniman, and Zink, 1961, p. 543).

After a number of years, the American public considered the educational provisions of the GI Bill such a huge success that one reasonably might contend that it "solved entirely" the problem under consideration. Very few government programs have had stronger public support, acclaim, and even adoration than this one. Following World War II and the Korean War, the GI Bill had almost no opposition. The GI Bill deserved this success by helping to educate an entire generation of young Americans, most of whom otherwise probably would not have gone to vocational school, let alone to college. The federal government paid full tuition and all fees (irrespective of the type of college or university), covered the cost of textbooks, and paid a monthly stipend ($75 per month for most veterans) to cover living expenses.

The program also provided for loans, subsidies, and other benefits. Nearly 8 million veterans of the war against the Axis took advantage of the educational provisions of the GI Bill. The program did have some problems, such as phony vocational and business schools, but these paled into insignificance compared to the widespread benefits that so many of our citizens derived and the enormous contributions these young people later made to their country. Subsequent GI bills, especially for Vietnam veterans and for the professional military, became controversial, and these veterans never enjoyed the largesse showered on veterans of World War II and the Korean War.

The GI Bill also provided for low-cost loans for veterans to purchase houses, enabling millions to own their own homes as they started their families after World War II. This financial assistance helped give rise to the growth of the suburbs in the United States.

Thalidomide Case (Column A)

The thalidomide episode tells how some highly skilled and motivated researchers at the U.S. Food and Drug Administration (FDA) took action that saved untold numbers of babies in the United States from serious limb deformities. By withholding approval of the sale of this drug in the United States, these scientists helped solve a very difficult and emotional medical policy issue, one fraught with moral and ethical questions (U.S. House, 1969).

In 1954, a Swiss firm first conceived of thalidomide as a promising pharmaceutical. After additional testing, the company abandoned the project. Several years later a West German company, Chemie Grunenthal G.m.b.H. of Stolberg marketed it as a sedative or sleep-inducing agent. The firm also thought that thalidomide could be useful in cases of epilepsy as an anticonvulsant. The drug proved worthless for epilepsy. However, it did induce sleep, and Grunenthal sold it for that purpose.

Pharmaceutical firms stated that people could take the drug in large doses without harmful effects. By 1960 it became Germany's most popular sleeping pill and tranquilizer. At one time or another, drug companies claimed that this inexpensive sedative could cure the grippe, neuralgia, and asthma and also could be used as a cough medicine. Of particular significance, European doctors believed that it was useful as an antiemetic in early pregnancy. The drug was sold in many countries under different brand names. Moreover, many other drugs incorporated thalidomide in their formulas. People had such faith in the drug that in some countries, such as West Germany, it could be bought without a prescription.

As sales soared, so did problems. No warnings appeared about adverse effects until the early 1960s. At that time, isolated reports began to circulate that thalidomide produced peripheral neuritis. A more serious side effect of thalidomide, however, also became apparent. Taken during the first three months of pregnancy, the drug had a 50–50 chance of producing phocomelia, an acute deformity, especially of the limbs. German physicians increasingly questioned the drug's use. In November 1961, Grunenthal withdrew the drug from the market, and two days later the West German government issued warnings about deformities in babies. This action came too late in Europe to prevent large and widespread physical and emotional consequences.

The FDA assigned Frances O. Kelsey, a serious and hardworking research scientist, the task of assessing thalidomide. Past research in the field led her to have doubts about the drug. She also read up-to-date reports indicating the drug's dangers. European newspapers first announced disturbing facts, which later appeared in the American press. In fact, a consensus later emerged that American journalism deserved much credit for alerting the nation to the perils of thalidomide. The FDA denied automatic approval of the manufacturer's application that would have taken place 60 days after submittal.

Kelsey repeatedly delayed approval by citing "insufficient data." An essential question arose: Did thalidomide contribute to human comfort and well-being enough to justify an evident, but imperfectly defined, medical need? By March 1961, the Merrell Company, the U.S. firm seeking to manufacture the drug, withdrew its application. Dr. Kelsey became a well-publicized hero. Some observers claimed that the United States enjoyed just pure luck because in this country women who took the drug in its experimental stage took it late in their pregnancy.

The thalidomide case triggered much public debate about government's responsibility in ensuring that only safe products enter the market at the earliest time possible. Undue haste can enable a product to reach customers before the FDA adequately could test it and judge it safe. On the other hand, unnecessary and prolonged government delays could deny to needy people products that could help cure them and make them comfortable. This case illustrates how some individuals in a regulatory arm of government completely solved a problem before it could cause havoc in the United States. Compared to the 10,000 birth defects and unknown number of miscarriages in Europe, less than two dozen cases of babies with missing or misshapen limbs occurred in the United States. One can conclude that FDA's caution just about solved the problem of thalidomide in the United States (John Schwartz, 1998).

The United States can take great pride in how it addressed the problem of thalidomide. Yet the speed with which new pharmaceuticals can enter the market remains a formidable question that will have to be solved on a case-by-case basis.

COPING

Although executives cannot conquer all problems, they need not easily accept failure or meekly submit to the will of others. They do have another major option, and this chapter discusses it.

Executives can cope with conditions rather than let matters remain static or grow worse. The word *cope* originated as a masonry term. It denotes the top layer of a brick or stone wall, usually built with a slope to shed water. Thus, the word means the strength that builders apply against forces opposing them. In coping, executives strenuously struggle against disagreeable and unwanted circumstances, usually with marginal (not dramatic) success. The importance of the word as used here signifies an effort to deal with problems but not actually doing away with them.

Coping often takes place when executives encounter turbulence in their undertakings. Turbulence happens when changes occur very rapidly, especially when the task at hand is very complex. Such is the case in the fields of information and communications. We are witnessing significant turbulence in the growth of these two interrelated mega industries that have come, perhaps more than any others, at the close of the century to propel the nation's economy (Chakravarthy, 1997). However, perhaps turbulence is the kind of problem we like to have if it means that a beneficial economic activity is growing.

When coping, executives should make all or some of several types of efforts. Above all, they have to display an emotional commitment, believing that in doing what they are doing they can make a difference. If these officials have lost faith in their abilities to hold their own, coping becomes a forlorn undertaking. Moreover, although emotional commitments might prove sufficient, in many instances, decisionmakers might have to be willing or able to apply resources in their undertakings. For example, without possessing minimum financial assets, a company fighting bankruptcy might find that it no longer can cope. Those striving to survive usually must possess a certain degree of intellectual endowment. They should be smart enough to discover ways to hold their own under adverse circumstances. Finally, executives must be able to devote sufficient time to the task. If too many matters simultaneously command their attention, they very well might lack the time to give all or most of them the attention that they deserve.

Job's Case (Column B)

The Old Testament tells several stories in which coping played a major role. No biblical tale has had a greater emotional and intellectual impact or is written in a more elegant, poetic style than the Book of Job. When God inflicted all sorts of sufferings on Job to test the man's faith, God's victim did not take his punishments lying down. Instead, he engaged in very serious coping with God.

Job leveled his anger at God's injustice and the evil that had befallen him. Job cries, "I swear by God, who has wronged me and filled my cup with despair, that while there is life in this body and as long as I can breathe, I will never let you convict me; I will never give up my claim. I will hold tight to my innocence; my mind will never submit" (Mitchell, 1987, p. 64).

To the end, Job continued to have faith in God's omniscience, power, and justice. He recognized the limits of his own mortality. He came to understand that God's ways remain mysterious and inscrutable; they lie beyond man's understanding but not beyond one's right to cope. In sum, Job submitted to God's will but not passively. Coping, very likely, assisted Job in influencing God to return the wealth and health that He had taken away. Yet Job clearly understood that God made that decision. All of Job's arguments in no way reduced the absolute power of God.

MCI Case (Column B)

In no other area have commercial firms resorted to coping more energetically and skillfully than in the communications industry. Microwave Communications Incorporated (MCI) and Sprint in the American communications industry undertook rigorous coping efforts. However, to save space and time, the discussion here is limited to MCI.

With the breakup of American Telephone and Telegraph (AT&T) in 1968, MCI offered new long-distance service (Mattera, 1987, pp. 73–74). MCI accurately saw as its major problem AT&T's domination of the long-distance telecommunications business. William McGowan, the cofounder of MCI, aimed above all to break up AT&T's monopoly (Moskowitz, Levering, and Katz, 1990). MCI convinced the Federal Communications Commission to open up the long-distance business to competition. MCI then built its own transmission facilities, chiefly a string of microwave tower networks. It rejected AT&T's attitude of pricing long-distance service as a luxury and concentrated on providing this service at substantially reduced rates (Drucker, 1985, p. 82). MCI could and did compete in a resolute and realistic way with AT&T.

The executives at AT&T took seriously this increased competition in a part of their business that produced an excellent source of revenue. MCI also benefitted from paying reduced fees to AT&T companies for local access. After years of legal wrangling, in 1980 the federal courts sided with MCI against AT&T, fortifying MCI's legal position. The subsequent breakup of AT&T put MCI on an equal legal footing with the telecommunications giant. By the mid-1980s, MCI acquired Telecom USA, the fourth-ranked American long-distance company, and became the second-ranked long-distance firm in the country.

MCI knew that to cope it had to institutionalize change to counter the natural tendency of organizations to become rigid. Living with the status quo would have prevented MCI from enlarging its share of the market. The firm exhibits vigor, energy, and barely controlled chaos, giving it the strength to advance on its competitors (Peters, 1992, p. 306).

AT&T and MCI conducted vigorous marketing programs, including extensive advertising to attract and retain customers. In 1985 alone these marketing programs cost some $500 million. By mid-1990 MCI had acquired 5 million customers, a large enough number that one could consider it a partial solution to MCI's problems. No doubt, a clientele this size could have come about only through major coping efforts by MCI. Despite all the resources that MCI poured into its coping effort, the firm could not budge AT&T from its dominant position. Many users displayed a natural resistance to making a change, and others were convinced that AT&T charged less. Still others became too bewildered to alter their behavior. They stayed with AT&T by default.

Although MCI captured some 12 percent of all U.S. long-distance business, it still ranked a low second. Thus, by the 1990s MCI could capture no more than a relatively small share of the total communications market. Later in the 1990s MCI increased its portion but did little to loosen AT&T's hold. MCI likewise came to earn an annual profit of some $500 million (a tidy sum for coping) but not one that put MCI anywhere near the leadership in the long-distance business.

If one assumes that MCI continues to work at becoming the largest firm in this field, either in the near or far future, it must intensify its coping efforts. MCI needs huge investments and other actions if it still wants to overtake AT&T. Even if MCI seems willing to settle for a comfortable second place, a major achievement in itself, its coping efforts will still require attention and resources. Although MCI can be proud of its record, as measured by the size of its accomplishments in the overall communications business, its coping efforts have been relatively modest.

ACCOMMODATION

As noted earlier, executives never become free of the need to solve the right problem. At times, they might not even have the determination, talent, skills, resources, or luck to make a discernible dent in abolishing unwanted circumstances. Said another way, they have no access to solutions that can improve a situation in a meaningful way. Under these circumstances, executives might be forced to accommodate to a less than desirable situation.

The word *accommodation* connotes living with or coming to terms with varying degrees of dissatisfaction. E.W. Burgess (1930, pp. 403–404) notes that the word first appeared in the social sciences in 1895. As used in this volume, the word *accommodation* means preventing events from worsening to a point at which decisionmakers can no longer bear the financial, human, political, or organizational costs.

In modern times, the most important message in business and government is "Don't fail." In its ultimate sense this injunction means not to allow a situation to grow significantly worse. Everyone knows that to survive, commercial enterprises must avoid a financial hemorrhage. They might not make a big profit, but they must limit losses to the sustainable until better times come along.

In analyzing the nature of large organizations, David Brown (1982, p. 180) noted, "By being willing to accommodate, we recognize that preserving a relationship is more important than the winning of a particular point." On the other hand, to the extent possible, through accommodation, CEOs seek to save as much of the favorable aspects of a bad situation as possible. By the very act of accommodating, they attempt to live with habits, attitudes, institutions, and values that they see as less than attractive but necessary. To do this, they must make trade-offs.

Some stalwarts hate the idea of accommodation (Baldwin, 1985). They see *accommodation* as another term for *weakness*. It does not, as its defenders suggest, really prevent the worst from occurring. Environmental zealots equate accommodations that environmental regulators have with private industry as "sellouts." Governments should not accommodate industry, allowing businesses to take halfway measures in cleaning up the air, land, and water. To those in the private sector, economic factors are the true guideposts of individual and social action. They counter that society has little choice but to accommodate to economic realities (e.g., jobs, industrial progress, foreign trade) even if it means compromising on or slowing down on antipollution programs. These skeptics argue that humanity gains little if it has pure air, clean rivers, and grand parks but loses well-paying jobs. Neither slums nor unattractive landfills are very desirable cures.

Belize Case (Column C)

Accommodation also has played a conspicuous role in international affairs. In settling border disputes peacefully, diplomats have to accommodate conflicting views and interests. For many years, Guatemala claimed the neighboring independent state of Belize in Central America as its "lost province." At times, it even has threatened military force to take back the territory. To counter this threat, Belize relies on a small British military force stationed in the country. (Belize was once a British colony.) In reality, Guatemala, Belize, and Great Britain have all accommodated to this unsatisfactory border situation for many years, learning to live with it. The likelihood of war over the Belize issue today remains remote ("Belize," 1990).

Blow-Mold Packers Case (Column C)

In the 1970s, Blow-Mold Packers Inc. (BMP), a producer of plastic containers, experienced considerable growth. After a few decades, the sweet picture turned sour. The firm comprised four divisions, all being run on a decentralized profit center basis. By the summer of 1969 top leadership had not yet decided on the exact role that the staff should play. For example, the president of the company ran the organization as a one-man show and lacked management control reports from his subordinates. In addition, professionals within the company all reported to the president (leading to a span-of-control problem). They also felt unsure of themselves and their responsibilities (Christensen, Andrews, and Bower, 1978, pp. 681–710).

Despite these deficiencies, the company generally performed adequately. Obviously, if BMP could improve the effectiveness of its line and staff personnel, it could increase its profits even more. As it turned out, the company improved its management to offset a slowdown in sales and profits.

In looking for a way out, BMP acquired additional firms, which required instant delegation of many responsibilities but did little to help the firm solve its fundamental management problems. The CEO still tried to run the company on the General Motors model with several divisions and with the aid of a central headquarters staff.

Unfortunately, this scheme failed, largely because of flaws in the company's personnel policies. The firm had to create, actually to hire, a corporate staff, a step that was premature because middle management was not prepared for it. BMP's executives did make some efforts that improved performance marginally. In addition to buying some new firms, its top executives hired a few effective executives. However, the company did not apply enough resources to enable it to do more than hold its own (i.e., to accommodate to circumstances).

SUMMARY

Executives obviously want to eradicate unsatisfactory situations. The GI Bill and thalidomide cases illustrate episodes in which they were able to do this. If the desired outcome proves impossible, impractical, onerous, or difficult (as is often the case), decisionmakers can choose less ambitious approaches, such as coping with or accommodating to existing problems. Coping sometimes brings about incremental improvements in the executive's lot. If executives still face demanding problems, they may have to learn to live with them.

CHAPTER 11

Perceived Outcomes

This last chapter examines the satisfactory and unsatisfactory conditions that decisionmakers believe result from the solutions that they apply. What kinds of outcomes do executives think they are fashioning? Sometimes they cannot identify these outcomes with precision and have to interpret the nature of the environment. All too often major solutions produce few durable and stable environments. Furthermore, inasmuch as individual decisionmakers have only limited control, extraneous factors can mask the results.

Figure 11.1 identifies three major perceived environments, listed according to degree of achievement. This spectrum runs from utopia (total success) to progress (varying degrees of success) to termination (no success, total failure, or bankruptcy in the commercial world).

During their lifetimes few enterprises or organizations run the full course sequentially from perfection to abandonment. Usually they show or fail to show progress.

UTOPIA

At first glance, serious discussions about utopian outcomes seem a flight of fancy, perhaps even folly. Theoretically, in such idyllic settings executives face no inadequacies, no ineptness, no disorder, no ineffectiveness, no rancor, no melancholia. In addition, total happiness also has a negative

Figure 11.1
Cases Illustrating Perceived Outcomes

Column A	Column B	Column C
Utopia *Perfection*	**Progress** *Improvement*	**Failure** *Bankruptcy/* *Abandonment/* *Termination*
•Hershey Case •Hewlett-Packard Case •Microsoft Case	•Abacus Case •Procter & Gamble Case •Volvo Case	•Pan Am Airlines Case •Supersonic Aircraft Case

side. It does not challenge executives in a way that calls for their best efforts. The executive never has to demonstrate administrative heroics.

Because perfection rarely exists, utopia resides mostly as an abstraction. Nevertheless, if executives believe that they work under such exceedingly favorable conditions, they tend to behave in certain ways. Thus, they should know some of utopia's core ideas.

No one thought more deeply and with greater clarity about this subject than Sir Thomas More (1478–1535). In his famous political satire *Utopia*, More described the nature and dynamics of what appeared to him to be the "best society" (Reynolds, 1968). In seeking the best, More bitterly attacked the traditional attitudes and practices of the ruling English nobility of his time. All too often this privileged group disregarded reason, relying instead on a tradition steeped in unjust prerogatives and inequality. To More, right, not wrong, exists within his utopia. Logic tells him that his visionary community solves the problem of crime by placing all criminals inside jails, leaving all the honest people outside jail. What could be more logical (or just)?

However, he did not fool himself. He wisely chose the Greek word *utopia*, meaning "no place," as the label for his faultless society. He seemed to suggest that if individuals know what constitutes an ideal community, they are better prepared in trying to achieve it and, in the process (even if they fail), to improve existing conditions.

Some decades later Sir Francis Bacon (1561–1626) contributed to the concept of utopia. He gave us new and worthwhile insights into the dynamics of a perfect society. In his *New Atlantis*, science became the key to prosperity, goodness, and happiness (Bacon, 1990, pp. 199–214). In his idyllic state of affairs, people depended upon new knowledge and the scientific method to eliminate problems. To Bacon, science served as a collaborative venture, conducted systematically and objectively, with the aim of perfecting humankind's material condition. Those who write about the utopian environment in which some modern institutions find themselves echo some of the thoughts of More and Bacon.

Hershey Case (Column A)

No entrepreneur believed more passionately that he had created a commercial utopia than did Milton S. Hershey, the founder of the Hershey Chocolate Company. In Figure 11.1 Hershey's perceived outcome is situated at the extreme left of the spectrum of imagined results. He believed that his firm produced a product unexcelled by any other candymaker and that the public already knew this. Having achieved the best, he saw no need to tamper with his products or with the packaging or with his sales methods. What's more, as long as his company maintained the status quo, his customers would recognize immediately the candy's worth and its highly distinctive wrappers.

In Pennsylvania, this entrepreneur built the world's largest chocolate factory in a city named for him. Guides conducted tours through the factory, and visitors looked with great anticipation for the free samples of chocolate distributed at the end of the tour. Hershey also founded a successful amusement park nearby, which attracted thousands of visitors. Hershey Park served as a forerunner of the theme parks that Disney and others built in the post–World War II period.

In such a rosy environment, this candymaker believed that he did not have to worry about competition. Feeling very confident, he ordered the firm to carry on no commercial advertising whatsoever ("Hershey," 1990). Hershey saw no need to spend money trying to convince potential customers of the value of his product when the public already had decided that his chocolates were best. When Hershey left the firm, his successors came to realize that their famous founder had believed in a myth that hurt the firm. Although Hershey's products were popular, the competition seemed ready to seize the opportunity to capture a larger share of the market. The new executives began to advertise.

Hewlett-Packard Case (Column A)

Another firm that many people came to regard as having a utopian nature arose in Silicon Valley, the heart of America's computer and information technology industry. Especially those who knew the computer industry intimately came to view Hewlett-Packard (H-P) as a first-rate firm. They believed that Bill Hewlett and Dave Packard were entrepreneurs and executives who ran an electronics/computer company as close to utopian standards as possible. During the Nixon administration, Dave Packard became a highly regarded executive in the Department of Defense, especially in the field of weapons acquisition.

Little doubt exists that over the years the firm's calculators and other specialized electronic instruments had earned a deservedly high reputation. Thomas Peters and Robert Waterman tell of having two young en-

gineers employed at H-P regale them for an hour with highly
complimentary stories about Hewlett and Packard, although these employees never had seen, let alone talked to, their CEOs (Peters and Waterman, 1982, p. 75).

Several reasons seem to account for such attitudes. First of all, the firm
grew during a period in which the public increasingly demanded technological, especially electronic, products. Because companies increasingly resorted to systematic analysis to solve their problems, they welcomed
cost-effective technologies and time-saving techniques. Hewlett-Packard
took advantage of this favorable market and produced just the right commercial items.

To gain the most from its workforce and market opportunities, the firm's
top leadership delegated authority as far down the line as possible. Executives kept in touch with the firm's workforce as well as with market
opportunities. Highly placed executives at H-P depended on the participation of people up and down its organizational chain to improve the
company's performance. This participation enabled H-P's personnel down
the line to keep abreast of problems and, thus, to know when and how to
try to solve them at the lowest possible level of decisionmaking.

At H-P busy bands of executives, supervisors, workers, engineers, and
salesmen met periodically in the division chief's office to identify problems
and debate controversies. Marketing agents anonymously sent pound
boxes of pistachio nuts to salesmen who sold new machines. The company's executives and employees shared many values, and H-P hired individuals who usually knew how to react to new situations. The firm's top
executives made certain that they periodically reported trends to the mem-
bership.

Like all business enterprises, over time H-P encountered certain difficulties. Tom Peters noted that although the firm for a time lost some luster
by centralizing too much, it took the necessary actions to correct that
mistake (Peters, 1992, pp. 288, 291). Neither this error nor any other seems
to have overtaxed the competence of its executives. The firm continues to
supply its market with high-quality products, maintaining its leadership in
almost utopian terms.

Microsoft Case (Column A)

By the last decade of the twentieth century, computerized information
systems triumphed, becoming a dominant factor of the age. Because of
the critical importance of software, needed to operate computers, Bill
Gates, the CEO of the company that developed software, earned a reputation that when it came to business decisions, he could do no wrong. To
him, newly developing cyberspace (bewilderingly diverse and geographi-
cally far-flung networks of corporations employing interdependent groups

of problem solvers) increasingly was influencing the way of doing business (Pruitt and Barrett, 1991, p. 438). "Gates speaks of a new stage of capitalism in which perfect information becomes the basis for the perfection of the market" (Dawson and Foster, 1996, p. 40). This statement snugly fits the description of a utopian environment. No doubt, by this remark, Gates meant a firm that could come up with an unending flow of innovative and useful ideas.

As the events of 1997 show, even utopia has its limitations. Microsoft's competitors accused Bill Gates of monopolistic practices. In 1998, the U.S. Department of Justice and a number of states sued Microsoft, accusing the firm of holding on to a preponderant position in the computer operating systems market by applying improper methods to gain its ends. This antitrust suit charged Gates with using unfit tactics to squash his competitors, especially the Netscape Web browser and Navigator. Microsoft engaged in incorrect, exclusionary conduct in several ways. The charge that drew the most attention was Microsoft's demand that consumers purchase Microsoft's Internet browser as a condition of buying Windows, its popular computer system. Government lawyers especially were asking the court to force Microsoft to do away with its exclusionary contracts. The government based its case on testimony from Microsoft's competitors and partners and internal e-mail messages that vividly showed the firm's competitive ends and the suggested improper means of attaining them.

Microsoft countered that the government had not proved its case. The company claimed that competitors, especially new firms, are constantly challenging its top position. Gates argued that consumers enjoyed a convenience from having Internet Explorer bundled into Windows. It seems that the testimony phase of the trial, begun in October 1998, was supposed to last until March 1999. Given the time for the trial judge to write an opinion, the trial phase should end in the summer of 1999. That opinion should have a major effect on Microsoft and the entire operating computer business. The losing side no doubt will appeal and, most likely, the U.S. Supreme Court will make the final decision. During this period, both Gates and his company certainly do not consider that they are enjoying utopia.

PROGRESS (IMPROVEMENT)

Obviously, there are limits to the validity of utopian thinking. Those who believe in a future information utopia are correct in thinking that the new technologies do resemble the printing press, in that they might have an effect on history. However, one easily could ascribe to them benefits well beyond their capabilities.

Human institutions then obviously succeed more often in achieving progress than in attaining utopias. By adopting sound ideas, working hard, and enjoying a little luck, their executives can leave conditions better off than they found them. Although people may never gain perfection, they can bring about important improvements through a process that we call "progress" ("Progress," 1990, pp. 349–356). They can do this because, as Auguste Comte and John Stuart Mill suggest, human relations are amenable to intelligent understanding, and thus people can see the better path (Sabine, 1950, p. 717).

Abacus Case (Column B)

It is well known that early in the space program Soviet scientists employed some of the world's most advanced technology in tackling difficult scientific and engineering problems. What is less well known is that the financial departments for the Soviet space program were using the ancient abacus to help them calculate their finances. The abacus, probably of Babylonian origin, saw widespread use during the Middle Ages and survives today in the Middle East, China, Japan, and the former Soviet Union (Smith, 1969, pp. 310–311).

Although the abacus certainly cannot calculate nearly as effectively as the modern, advanced computer, on the whole, financial staffs face the kinds of calculation tasks that they can do well enough with this older instrument. In fact, some argue that in the hands of an expert practitioner the abacus can compete against some modern mechanical calculating machines. We must consider the use of the abacus in Soviet financial administration in the early years of space exploration as true "progress" compared to what was available in low-technology societies. Early in the space age, financial offices in the Soviet Union were low-technology communities. Some other low-technology groups did not even have an abacus but depended on memory and mental calculations. In some instances, such groups could take advantage of the contemporary use of pencil and paper and could resort to the even more primitive method of counting by fingers, stones, or other objects (Durant, 1954b, p. 79).

Procter & Gamble Case (Column B)

Procter & Gamble (P&G), one of the world's largest and most successful producers of soaps, detergents, toothpaste, and similar consumer products, seemed generally satisfied with its market performance. The firm enjoyed great success in its efforts to diversify, becoming a producer of disposable diapers (Drucker, 1973, p. 701). For this reason, it enjoyed major progress and a healthy profit picture. In general, fate had been kind to Procter & Gamble. The American public increasingly had become conscious of cleanliness and health. As a result, P&G's products were in demand. The firm's top executives took advantage of an already favorable market to make even more progress.

The entrepreneurs at P&G insisted on conducting high-quality analyses before making major decisions, adding greatly to the strength of the company. The company developed an excellent data base, illuminating the problems associated with its markets and competitors. To simplify matters, P&G's leaders sought to eliminate paperwork; its insistence on one-page memoranda became a legend in the business world. Everyone at P&G knew that a high-quality product remained the sine qua non of the company's success. From the very outset, P&G's leaders recognized that the interests of the organization could not be separated from the interests of its employees. P&G seriously encouraged healthy competition among its brand managers.

Although the firm prospered, its status could not be called utopian. No matter how thoughtful P&G's leaders were and despite how well they went about solving their problems, economic circumstances in the late 1980s and early 1990s forced P&G to reduce the size of its workforce and executive staffs. P&G's policy of encouraging competition among brands generally proved worthwhile; however, as Tom Peters notes, "The P&G model, for example, has blemishes. Chief among them: Even the 'cannibals' at P&G—brands attacking other brands in the same family—frequently become big, bureaucratic, and dull" (1992, p. 526).

Nonetheless, because P&G executives knew how to run a company effectively, they continued to make progress in overcoming inadequate situations and bringing them up to tolerable levels.

Volvo Case (Column B)

Volvo, a major automobile manufacturer in Sweden, experienced the fate of a firm that enjoyed some, but not dramatic, improvement in trying to fix its problems. Volvo became an independent corporation in 1935. It supplied Sweden with most of its motor cars for many years. The firm manufactured its products in Sweden and in subsidiaries abroad. In 1978 a state-owned Norwegian holding company acquired 40 percent of Volvo's stock. A Swedish holding company held the remaining 60 percent. Consequently, Volvo assumed the unique position of being owned by two governments.

The company chiefly aimed to sell medium-sized passenger cars. It took pride in the very favorable reputation it had earned for the conservative designs, high-quality engineering, comfort, and safety of its cars. Although Sweden remained the company's largest single market, in the 1980s exports accounted for more than three-fourths of its revenue.

At that time, Volvo realized that it had to strengthen its competitive position if it wanted to hold its own, especially against the rising tide of Japanese automobile exports (Oster, 1991) and also cars manufactured at American-owed plants in Europe. At first, Swedish automobile executives responded by convincing European governments to set quotas, thereby freezing Japanese exports at then-current levels.

Volvo's decisionmakers estimated that in the future American firms operating in Europe, such as General Motors and Ford, would continue to maintain their combined 24 percent share of the European market. The four European automobile companies most likely would experience major declines in sales as Japanese competition grew. These four European firms were Volkswagen (West Germany), Renault (France), Peugeot (France), and Fiat (Italy) (Toffler, 1980, p. 70).

Volvo had good reasons for contemplating a harsh future if it could not reinforce its competitive position both at home and abroad. The statistics did not reassure the company. In 1989, it took a European car producer 36.2 hours to build a car; the United States spent 25.1 hours and the Japanese 16.8 hours. In other words, it took the Europeans more than twice as long to manufacture a car as it took their Japanese rivals. Other relevant statistics also troubled the firm's executives. European manufacturers encountered 176 problems per 100 vehicles, compared to 153 for the United States and 114 for Japan.

By the early 1990s uncontrollable events caused additional problems. First and foremost, the European Economic Community (the Common Market or the EEC) experienced greater integration, and the firms located outside EEC found themselves at a disadvantage. Volvo now had to play by tough regional rules rather than by the cozy arrangements that European carmakers previously had set up for themselves.

Despite the coming of the Common Market, European companies initially found that most or all of their products still sold in the home market. Nonetheless, Europe's automobile industries could not prevent Japanese exports from capturing a significant share of the market. Volvo still had to contend with the fierce Japanese competition. Volvo's profits plummeted as its sales throughout Europe declined sharply (Berggren, 1992).

As already noted, the Japanese produced automobiles more efficiently than their European rivals. Moreover, they manufactured a high-quality product. In addition, Japanese firms sold their cars at favorable prices, compared to their Swedish, European, or American rivals. Volvo executives knew that their outdated machine tools and other antiquated equipment drove up their manufacturing costs. Japanese manufacturers consumed fewer man-hours to design a car from the ground up than did their European and U.S. competitors.

On the average, Japanese firms produced new versions of their cars every 4.5 years, compared to every 8 years for the United States and somewhat longer for European companies. Volvo decided to automate its production process as much as possible in an attempt to protect the company's share of the market. In its effort to counter Japanese imports, the firm upgraded the plant and equipment on its production line, including using robots, computers, software, and other automated machines.

To a considerable extent Volvo's efforts succeeded. For example, Volvo automated about 95 percent of its facility at Born and spent $72 million modernizing the paint shop there, introducing advanced robots and automatic sprayers. This new equipment could apply 22 treatments to each car body. To improve spot welding, the company installed 125 robots at Born's body shop, enabling that facility to reduce the number of workers who earned $18,000 a year. At its Torslanda plant near Gothenburg, Sweden, Volvo introduced an automated welding line, reducing the number of workers from 100 to 20 over two shifts (Szyliowicz, 1981, pp. 253–254). In the 1980s the firm considered installing a fully computerized production system, covering both body construction and finishing; this technology would cut the number of employees enormously.

Volvo also attempted to induce its labor force to participate in decisionmaking from the early design stage to the final manufacturing phase. This project backfired. Instead of energizing employees to perform more effectively, it actually made workers uncertain about their role in the production process. In other words, workers and managers at Volvo found it hard to adopt Japanese techniques.

Volvo did join with the Japanese firm Mitsubishi with the aim of producing a competitive automobile. Volvo's leaders had asked themselves, Would joint development and production with a major Japanese automobile firm improve Volvo's overall position? Mitsubishi, founded in 1873, entered into this arrangement because it wanted to obtain its first manufacturing facility in Europe and to do it rather cheaply. The Japanese also wanted to learn how Volvo built its high-quality and safe cars.

Volvo had to fix some knotty problems to make the joint venture a success. Mitsubishi estimated that Volvo had to cut its labor force by 20 percent in order to attain leaner production. Volvo might have to sell some of its factories and foundries to third parties, shifting some 1,300 workers to companies that paid smaller salaries. In learning the Mitsubishi system, Volvo executives and workers encountered language problems. They had to shift from communicating in Swedish and Dutch to using English as the common language.

Volvo's workers also had difficulties in understanding the Japanese interpretation of acceptable quality levels and quality "circles." "Circles" are groups of employees assigned to a particular operation who meet together on the factory floor where they discuss their missions and activities with the aim of improving performance (D. Brown, 1982, pp. 277–278; Ouchi, 1981, pp. 261–268). Peters and Waterman call quality circles "gimmicks" that although valid can act as smokescreens. Executives could show no intense interest and could continue to get away with really not doing their avowed job of involving people (Peters and Waterman, 1982, p. 241).

In terms of the "problem exchange ratio," Volvo was facing more serious problems as the decade of the 1990s opened. After taking some very expensive actions, the company's executives found that although they had improved Volvo's production capacities, they had not solved their chief problem: preventing Japanese automobile manufacturers from capturing a sizable share of the market. Nonetheless, Volvo had countered threats to its survival. It still remained a major automobile producer in Sweden and Europe, and it had improved its manufacturing and sales capabilities.

FAILURE (BANKRUPTCY/ABANDONMENT/ TERMINATION)

Circumstances beyond the control of decisionmakers or perhaps their ineptitude sometimes lead them to failure (Whyte, 1991). They find that they have to end a project prematurely, terminate a program, and sometimes abandon an entire enterprise. Such terminations obviously cause great hardship to employees and their families. People, including executives, experience hard times when they lose their jobs.

We all have heard about corporate failures in particular industries during certain times in the United States. For example, in the years following World War II, in the automobile industry, Nash, Hudson, LaSalle, Desoto, Kaiser-Frazier, Studebaker, and Packard all went out of business. By the end of the twentieth century, all locally owned and operated department stores in the Washington, D.C. area either disappeared altogether or were bought out by large, national merchandising corporations. The discussion here is limited to a brief reprise of two major decisions to end ongoing activities. In the first case Pan American Airlines, a major corporation, went out of business. In the second case, the U.S. government decided to terminate the development of the commercial supersonic transport.

Pan Am Case (Column C)

In going out of business, no company made more blazing headlines than Pan American World Airlines (Pan Am), the pioneer in international aviation. Its longtime director, Juan Trippe, had earned a reputation as a successful executive who nurtured the company from infancy to maturity. Yet, upon close inspection, one can spot the airline's major mistakes.

Some companies fail because they don't detect their precise problem or because their "solutions" do not work. Pan Am failed for both reasons. In January 1991, this airline, once a symbol of the United States to the world, filed for bankruptcy, seeking protection from its creditors. In effect, it went out of business ("Pan Am Seeks Chapter 11 Shield, Gets UAL-Backed Cash Infusion," 1991, p. A3).

Trippe, a colorful individual, financial wizard, and astute entrepreneur (Bender and Altschul, 1982), founded the airline in 1927. In the 1920s, he put together a group of financial backers who by 1930 converted a small mail-carrying line into the world's largest and the United States's oldest airline. Pan Am's clippers not only spanned the Atlantic, but the company built airfields on small Pacific islands so that amphibious aircraft could refuel on the seven-day, 8,200-mile flight between San Francisco and Manila.

Over the years, certain factors in international aviation created a less hospitable environment for Pan Am. First, after World War II, Pan Am began to confront some meaningful competition on its worldwide routes (Sampson, 1984, pp. 105–132). By the late 1940s, Transworld Airlines (TWA) started to fly the Atlantic, and United Airlines extended its routes to Hawaii. Both of these airlines also flew domestic routes, which they could use to feed their international business. After World War II every nation in the world seemingly established its own airline. These foreign companies enjoyed major advantages such as subsidies. Pan Am received no government largesse and had to compete for every dollar it earned. Foreign carriers continued flying, no matter how dismal their economic performance.

Second, if Pan Am wanted to land in overseas destinations, the United States had to grant the foreign airlines permission to land in the United States, thus strengthening the competition.

Third, in the early 1970s, the price of oil began to soar, adding huge costs to operating transport aircraft, especially Pan Am's jumbo jets. Once the price of fuel began to skyrocket, it never again became an inexpensive item in the cost structure of the airline industry.

Fourth, Pan Am felt the effects of the Airline Deregulation Act of 1978, which removed route-regulating authority from the federal government (Sampson, 1984, p. 136). Now each airline set its own fares and could choose those routes that promised the highest profits. Even during the period of government regulation, Pan Am's maneuverings in Washington could not stop other airlines from competing against some of Pan Am's most profitable routes.

Fifth, a series of recessions in various parts of the world decreased business in general. The airlines suffered the same downturn as other business sectors. Some of these recessions became serious and lasted a long time.

Sixth, Iraq's invasion of Kuwait and the subsequent Persian Gulf War caused potential passengers to cancel or delay their travel plans, producing a sharp drop in travel to the Middle East and a reduction in Pan Am's revenues.

Seventh, on top of all these problems came a searing blow. On December 28, 1988, Pan Am Flight 103 blew up over Lockerbie, Scotland, killing 270 people. As a result, the company faced many lawsuits. Pan Am tried to remedy some of its major problems, but the Lockerbie tragedy, time and again, came to haunt it, inducing some passengers to fly on other airlines.

Along with other airlines, Pan Am cut fares during the 1980s. These cuts enabled airlines, including Pan Am, to earn relatively well during the decade. By 1990, however, a drop in passenger revenues added to Pan Am's financial woes and prompted its decision to ask for additional fare reductions.

Some mention of the shift to jumbo jets seems appropriate here. Pan Am's leadership decided that the firm's declining financial status arose because its aircraft flew too few passengers. The Boeing 707/320 transport could only carry about 160 passengers, preventing the company from enjoying economies of scale. Trippe wanted a much larger carrier. Thus, Pan Am bought from Boeing the very expensive 747 jumbo jet, which could transport three times the number of passengers as the 707 and which would fly 10 percent faster, shaving 25 minutes from the New York to London run. Businessmen especially liked the fact that the operating costs per seat mile of the 747 would be 30 percent less than the 707. Trippe guessed correctly that passengers would prefer flying on these wide-bodied aircraft. The extra space meant a more comfortable ride, and the 25-minute savings appealed to many passengers.

Yet Pan Am failed to gain much of the anticipated economic advantages. Travelers did not flock to the new aircraft in the large numbers that Trippe had expected. These huge aircraft crossed the Atlantic with many empty seats (Sampson, 1984, p. 127). In effect, introducing the 747s simply aggravated an existing financial crisis, made worse by exorbitant fuel costs. The gains that Trippe had anticipated did not take place because of the disappointing number of passengers on the jumbo jets. In addition, Pan Am began to experience major flaws in the operations of the airline. For example, in August 1986 Pan Am agreed to pay nearly $2 million in fines to settle charges that it had violated various federal safety regulations.

Pan Am had no domestic routes to feed its international flights, a recognized major deficiency. However, its executives failed to identify correctly the type of domestic route structure that the airline needed. In 1979 Trippe bought National Airlines to obtain its domestic routes. The merger helped very little (Peters and Waterman, 1982, p. 299). National Airlines served the East Coast, carrying passengers chiefly between New York and Florida. It did connect the West Coast (California) to the East Coast (Florida) by a southern transcontinental route. However, few passengers used this route. Just as important, it failed to provide connections between the airline's East and West Coast terminals and interior cities (Bender and

Altschul, 1982, p. 254). In a last desperate attempt to increase profits, Pan Am inaugurated shuttle service between Washington, D.C. and New York in competition with Eastern Airlines. This move proved less than satisfactory.

Until very late in the game, Pan Am's leadership failed to identify a problem that should never have arisen in the first place. Throughout most of Pan Am's life it enjoyed a sterling reputation among its customers. As troubles mounted, its reputation suffered among America's flying public. Passengers complained of an arrogant attitude and indifference on the part of flight crews. Customers grumbled about poor service aboard the aircraft and the inflexibility of ticketing agents.

Trippe directed the company in an imperious style, often concealing his ideas and ambitions even from his top subordinates. Over the years he became increasingly inaccessible. Moreover, Trippe gave little thought to the firm's leadership in the future. He could not imagine Pan Am without him at the helm. Therefore, he paid almost no attention to the problem of the person to succeed him. Finally in 1968, Trippe announced that he planned to retire soon. He named Harold Gray to succeed him as chairman and chief executive officer and Najeeb Halaby as president. Gray acknowledged existing problems such as that of the 747 contract with Boeing. He called it "a mess" (Bender and Altschul, 1982, pp. 254, 515). Sick with cancer, he retired and turned his office over to Halaby. The new CEO instituted several purges and a program to improve the psychological conditions within the organization. His critics argued that his psychological efforts actually led to a companywide depression. Bombarded with criticism, Halaby resigned in 1972.

At the start of the decade, Pan Am's future was bleak. The airline reported that traffic declined 7.7 percent to 2.18 billion revenue passenger miles from 2.36 billion miles a year earlier ("Pan Am's December Traffic Fell," 1991, p. A4). It later reported that in January 1991 traffic fell 18.3 percent to 1.89 billion revenue passenger miles from 2.31 billion a year earlier ("Pan Am to Cut Its Work Force by 15% and Further Reduce Service to Europe," 1991, p. A5). By April, United Airlines and then American Airlines took over Pan Am's route between Miami and London. By April, revenue passenger miles fell to 1.7 billion ("Pan Am Unit's Traffic Declines," 1991, p. C5).

Pan Am began to sell the airline's profitable assets, such as the New York headquarters building and the Intercontinental Hotels chain. The unions became restive and a series of strikes and walkouts took place. The demise of the airline had a traumatic effect on its employees. Following the airline's bankruptcy, Pan Am's workers reported an increase in stress-related illness ("Lost Horizons: A Grand Tradition Can Make a Fall That Much Harder," 1991, p. A1).

In 1985, Pan Am had to sell its historical routes in the Pacific, its route to Germany, and the shuttle service (Moskowitz, Levering, and Katz, 1990, pp. 368–440, 559–560). In November 1991, Pan Am flew its last flight to Europe, marking the end of an era in which this American airline opened up the sky paths of the world to a huge number of people flying for business and pleasure ("Deregulation Blues: Pan Am Clipper," 1991, p. A12).

With a little hindsight, any observer of the airline industry could tell that Pan Am was attempting to operate a large, global, first-class airline with insufficient resources and with less than fully alert, creative, and dynamic executives.

The SST Case (Column C)

The U.S. supersonic transport (SST) case illustrates the termination of a specific project. Interestingly enough, this failure did relatively little harm to its parent commercial backer, the Boeing Company. Boeing continued as the leading manufacturer of commercial subsonic transports in the world and went on making a good living.

In the 1960s, the firm invested a considerable sum of its own funds to design an economic SST. The U.S. government awarded a contract to Boeing for developing the Mach 3 transport. Yet the SST came of age not in the United States but in England and France. British Airways and Air France pooled their efforts to develop the Concorde (Pauly, 1976). This aircraft, flying at Mach 2 (1,920 miles per hour) began transatlantic service in 1978. The Concorde, however, could not accommodate enough passengers and consumed too much expensive fuel to become truly profitable. It continues to operate because of the national prestige that France and Great Britain derive from it. No plans exist today anywhere for building another commercial SST.

From 1963 to 1971 the U.S. government spent more than $1 billion on its SST project. U.S. industry lacked the resources to build a profitable SST on its own. Thus, government assistance became mandatory. Critics strongly cautioned against inevitable environmental damage from huge quantities of noxious emissions. In addition, the engines of the SST made much more noise than the subsonic plane. Moreover, its sonic booms caused great disturbances in populated areas.

Scientists, some working on committees at the White House, emerged as perhaps the loudest and most articulate opponents. They pulled a lot of weight with Congress and with the public. Other detractors arose from the public at large and from interest groups. Most important, developers failed to make the SST an economically viable vehicle. The SST might have bypassed other difficulties but not one of being uneconomical. Congress's skepticism in 1971 led it to cut off all funds, killing the program.

Of interest, the Soviet Union also built a supersonic transport, the Tupolev TU-144, which went into commercial service in 1975. However, serious problems with the aircraft forced the Soviets to withdraw it from service in 1983. Aircraft manufacturers today focus on designing subsonic transports that consume less fuel.

SUMMARY

This chapter examines one type of outcome that results from decisions taken by executives—the environments that color the thinking of those working in institutions affected by the solutions that executives apply to problems. The ultimate outcome could be an environment that projects either (1) a utopian mind-set, (2) an outlook emphasizing progress whereby private firms and public agencies improve their performances by a discernible measure, or (3) a total failure and disappearance of a project, a program, or an institution.

More and Bacon provided the fundamental idea of the utopian concept; the Hershey, Hewlett-Packard, and Microsoft cases exemplified experiences that to individuals within those companies and to some outside observers seemed like utopia.

For its time, the abacus represented an improvement that helped people perform calculations more effectively than earlier devices. Procter & Gamble and Volvo also represent improvement, although important problems were left to be solved.

Failure obviously represents the least desirable outcome. It can bring about the end of an industrial development such as the SST or the bankruptcy of a once powerful company such as Pan Am.

Summary

As its chief message, this volume posits that decisionmakers and executives obviously assume, as one of their major tasks, discovering what they and their organizations are doing wrong. Executives naturally want to eliminate unwanted, unsatisfactory situations, replacing them with more favorable ones. At the start, they should take care first to identify their problems as accurately and precisely as possible. Such action gives them a better chance to address problems in an intelligent manner. *Above all, executives should aim to avoid expending great energies and resources in fashioning intelligent solutions, only to discover that these remedies address the wrong problem.* Furthermore, analysts have come up with a host of techniques for solving problems but have neglected to invent a large number of techniques for identifying problems.

Most of Part I (Chapters 1–8) advanced knowledge concerning the executive's tasks in acquiring, arranging, and analyzing data and other forms of information. Decisionmakers must find a means to break through the outer layers of information bases and then tap its appropriate facts, data, and opinions. Modern computers, ancillary electronic hardware, and communications equipment have vastly increased the ability of decisionmakers to obtain the information that they need. Although a huge amount of information has become available, within this mass the task of targeting a single item of needed information has grown more difficult. They may find that the information is either well ordered or chaotic (usually raw data that have not been processed into a logical arrangement). Naturally, it is harder to work with chaotic information than with well-arranged data.

In performing their jobs, executives must become aware of unwanted situations. In their efforts to identify problems, people have to acknowledge the differences in known (problems that they know), unknown (problems that they know that they don't know), and unknown unknown problems (problems that they don't know that they don't know). The third-mentioned type of problem remains the least understood and the most difficult to address.

Part II (Chapters 9–11) emphasized the outcome of solutions and decisions, especially the "problem exchange ratio" concept. Executives should understand that a problem rarely exists as a single entity but usually comprises a number of what this study labels "component problems." Executives can accomplish any of three results when applying solutions to component problems: (1) They can solve the entire problem, (2) they can solve some of the problem (leaving some components unsolved), or (3) they can create new component problems.

Consequently, after trying a solution, executives should compare the gravity of a problem at specific intervals over time. They can learn how well or poorly they have performed by using the PER. In applying the PER, executives attempt to assess the value of remedies at selected milestones by balancing the component problems that have been solved against the total problems remaining. The higher the ratio of component problems solved to total problems remaining (including the new problems that solutions generate), the more executives can come out ahead (or vice versa). By examining the PER at various milestones, decisionmakers can determine if they are coming out ahead (making progress), standing still, or making the situation worse.

In the smallpox and 360 computer cases, decisionmakers just about eradicated the problems. In the War on Cancer and Xerox cases, some of the problems were solved, but the unsolved problems that remained caused challenging conditions. In the Chamberlain case the new problems proved disastrous, and in the Green Revolution case, despite outstanding progress, farmers still had to contend with some serious problems that remained.

If decisionmakers cannot solve their problems, they still have other options available. They can cope with or accommodate to the unwanted circumstances that remain. In the case of Job, this biblical figure argued fiercely with God; in the MCI case, this firm fought fiercely to acquire a significant portion of the long-distance business from AT&T. In the Belize and Blow-Mold cases, the antagonists learned to live with an undesirable situation. In assessing the success or failure of various enterprises, one sees that their ultimate outcomes can resemble either a utopian environment, a progressing situation, or one in which an organization (e.g., a private firm or government agency) disappears or a program or a project ends. In the Hershey and Hewlett-Packard cases, the CEOs seemed to live in the best of all possible worlds. In the abacus, Procter & Gamble, and the Volvo cases, their history shows progress. In the Pan Am and SST cases, their executives had to terminate their efforts.

Readers would profit from exploring the following three principles:

• Executives suffer because although their literature pays ample attention to problem solving, it largely neglects problem identification—an equally important subject.

• Selected solutions can produce successful, indeterminate, or unsuccessful outcomes. Executives find this out by identifying the gravity of problems both before and after they have tried solutions. Obviously, those in charge hope that their solutions result in successful outcomes, but they cannot count on it.

• If solutions do not bring about satisfactory results, executives have available other options, such as coping and accommodation.

References

Ackoff, Russell. 1978. *The Art of Problem Solving*. New York: John Wiley & Sons.

Adams, James L. 1979. *Conceptual Blockbusting: A Guide to Better Ideas*, 2nd ed. New York: W.W. Norton.

Albert, Kenneth J., ed. 1980. *Handbook of Business Problem Solving*. New York: McGraw-Hill.

Alberts, David S., and Daniel S. Papp, eds. 1997. *The Information Age: An Anthology on Its Impacts and Consequences*, Vol. 1, Part 1. Washington, D.C.: National Defense University, Advanced Concepts, Technologies, and Information Strategies Institute for National Strategic Studies.

Alberts, David S., Daniel S. Papp, and W. Thomas Kemp III. 1997. "The Technologies of the Information Revolution." In David S. Alberts and Daniel S. Papp, eds., *The Information Age: An Anthology on Its Impacts and Consequences*, Vol. 1, Part 1, pp. 83–116. Washington, D.C.: National Defense University, Advanced Concepts, Technologies, and Information Strategies Institute for National Strategic Studies.

Alden, Jay. 1994. *Administration Course 650: Organizational Decision Making*. Washington, D.C.: National Defense University.

Alden, Jay. 1997. *Executive Decisionmaking Strategies*. Washington, D.C.: National Defense University, Information Resource Management College.

Allison, Graham T. 1971. *Essence of Decision: Explaining the Cuban Missile Crisis*. Boston: Little, Brown.

American Heritage Dictionary of the English Language, 3rd ed. 1992. Boston: Houghton Mifflin.

Andriole, Stephen J. 1983. *Handbook of Problem-Solving: An Analytical Methodology*. New York: Petrocelli Books.

Arkes, Hal R., and Kenneth R. Hammond. 1986. *Judgment and Decision Making: An Interdisciplinary Reader*. Cambridge, England: Cambridge University Press.

Arnold, John D. 1992. *The Complete Problem Solver: A Total System for Competitive Decision Making*. New York: John Wiley & Sons.

Axelrod, R., ed. 1976. *Structure of Decision: The Cognitive Maps of Political Elites*. Princeton, N.J.: Princeton University Press.

Bacon, Francis. 1990. "New Atlantis." In Mortimer J. Adler, ed., *Great Books of the Western World*, Vol. 28, pp. 199–214. Chicago: University of Chicago Press.

Baird, Bruce. 1978. *Introduction to Decision Analysis*. Boston: Duxbury Press.

Baird, Bruce F. 1989. *Managerial Decisions Under Uncertainty: An Introduction to the Analysis of Decision Making*. New York: John Wiley & Sons.

Baldwin, James Mark. 1985. *Mental Development in the Child and the Race*. New York: Macmillan.

Baranson, Jack. 1978. *Technology and the Multinationals: Corporate Strategies in a Changing World Economy*. Lexington, Mass.: Lexington Books/D.C. Heath.

Barber, Bernard. 1962. *Science and the Social Order*. New York: Collier Books.

Basiuk, Victor. 1977. *Technology, World Politics and American Policy*. New York: Columbia University Press.

Bazerman, Max H. 1986. *Judgment in Managerial Decision Making*. New York: John Wiley & Sons.

Beach, Lee Ray, and Terence R. Mitchell. 1978. "A Contingency Model for the Selection of Decision Strategies." *Academy of Management Review*, Vol. 3, No. 3, July, pp. 439–449.

"Belize," article in *Encyclopaedia Britannica*. 1990. Chicago: Encyclopaedia Britannica.

Bender, Marylin, and Selig Altschul. 1982. *The Chosen Instrument: The Rise and Fall of an American Entrepreneur*. New York: Simon & Schuster.

Bennett, Earl Dean, Floyd S. Brandt, and Charles R. Klasson. 1974. *Administrative Policy: Cases in Managerial Decision Making*, pp. 306–315. Columbus, Ohio: Charles E. Merrill.

Berggren, Christian. 1993. *Alternatives to Lean Production: Work Organization in the Swedish Auto Industry*. Ithaca, N.Y.: ILR Press.

Bernard, Chester I. 1968. *The Functions of the Executive*. Cambridge, Mass.: Harvard University Press.

Blalock, Hubert M. 1960. *Social Statistics*. New York: McGraw-Hill.

Blalock, Hubert M. 1970. *An Introduction to Social Research*. Englewood Cliffs, N.J.: Prentice-Hall.

Borchrave, Arnaud, and Michael Ledeen. 1980. "Selling Russia the Rope." *Fortune*, December 13, pp. 13–17.

Bowen, Howard R. 1969. "Why Are Businessmen Concerned About Their Social Responsibilities?" In Max D. Richards and William A. Nielander, eds., *Readings in Management*, 3rd ed., pp. 72–74. Cincinnati, Ohio: South-Western.

Bradley, D.J. 1990. "The Creation of IBM PC." *BYTE*, September, pp. 414–418.

Brightman, Richard W. 1971. *Information Systems for Modern Management.* New York: Macmillan.

Brown, David. 1982. *Managing the Large Organization: Issues, Ideas, Precepts, Innovations.* Mt. Airy, Md.: Lomond Books.

Brown, David S. 1989. *Management Concepts and Practices.* Washington, D.C.: National Defense University.

Brown, Fred R., ed. 1977. *Management: Concepts and Practice,* 4th ed. Mt. Airy, Md.: Lomond Books.

Brownstone, D.M., and G. Carruth. 1979. *Where to Find Business Information: A Worldwide Guide for Everyone Who Needs the Answers to Business Questions.* New York: John Wiley & Sons.

Burger, Edward J. 1980. *Science at the White House: A Political Liability.* Baltimore, Md.: Johns Hopkins University Press.

Burgess, E.W. "Accommodation," article in E.R.A. Seligman, ed., *Encyclopaedia of the Social Sciences,* Vol. 1. 1930. New York: Macmillan.

"Burgess, E.W.," article in E.R.A. Seligman, ed., *Encyclopaedia of the Social Sciences.* Vol. 1. 1930. New York: Macmillan.

"Bush's Address on the War in the Persian Gulf." 1991. *Facts on File,* Vol. 51, No. 2617, January 17, p. 28.

Campbell, Andrew, and Marcus Alexander. 1997. "What's Wrong with Strategy?" *Harvard Business Review,* November–December, pp. 42–51.

Carson, Rachel L. 1962. *Silent Spring.* Boston: Houghton Mifflin.

"Cease-fire Holds in Persian Gulf." 1991. *Facts on File,* Vol. 51, No. 2624, March 7, p. 156.

Chakravarthy, Bala. 1997. "A New Strategy Framework for Coping with Turbulence." *Sloan Management Review,* Vol. 38, No. 2, pp. 6–82.

Christensen, C. Roland, Kenneth R. Andrews, and Joseph L. Bower. 1978. *Business Policy: Text and Cases.* Homewood, Ill.: Irwin.

Christensen, C. Roland, Kenneth R. Andrews, Joseph L. Bower, Richard H. Hammermesh, and Michael Porter. 1987. *Business Policy: Text and Cases.* Homewood, Ill.: Irwin.

Churchill, Winston. 1948. *The Gathering Storm.* Cambridge, Mass.: Houghton Mifflin.

Churchman, L.W., R.L. Ackoff, and E.L. Arnoff. 1957. *Introduction to Operations Research.* New York: John Wiley & Sons.

Collis, David, and Cynthia A. Montgomery. 1998. "Creating Corporate Advantage." *Harvard Business Review,* May–June, pp. 71–83.

Cornell, Alexander. 1980. *The Decisionmaking Handbook.* Englewood Cliffs, N.J.: Prentice-Hall.

Dawson, Michael B., and John B. Foster. 1996. "Virtual Capitalism: The Political Economy of the Information Highway." *Monthly Review,* Vol. 48, No. 3, March, p. 40.

Delaney, William A. 1982. *The 30 Most Common Problems in Management and How to Solve Them.* New York: AMACOM.

de Madariaga, Salvador. 1948. *The Fall of the Spanish American Empire.* New York: Macmillan.

"Deregulation Blues: Pan Am Clipper." 1991. *Wall Street Journal,* November 21, p. A12.

Dewey, John. 1910. *How We Think*. New York: D.C. Heath.

Divine, Robert A., ed. 1971. *The Cuban Missile Crisis*. Chicago: Quadrangle Books.

Driver, Michael J., K.R. Brousseau, and P.L. Hunsaker. 1993. *The Dynamic Decision Maker*. San Francisco: Jossey-Bass.

Drucker, Peter. 1954. *The Practice of Management*. New York: Harper & Row.

Drucker, Peter. 1969. "The Objectives of a Business." In Max D. Richards and William Nierlander, eds., *Readings in Management*, 3rd ed., pp. 306–309. Cincinnati, Ohio: South-Western.

Drucker, Peter. 1973. *Tasks, Responsibilities, Practices*. New York: Harper & Row.

Drucker, Peter. 1993. *Management: Tasks, Practices, and Responsibilities*. New York: Harper Business.

Drucker, Peter. 1985. *Innovation and Entrepreneurship: Practice and Principles*. New York: Harper & Row.

"Drugs and Alcohol," article in *Grolier Encyclopaedia of Knowledge, Annual*. 1997. Danbury, Conn.: Grolier.

Durant, Will. 1954a. "The Life of Greece." *The Story of Civilization: Part II*. New York: Simon & Schuster.

Durant, Will. 1954b. "Our Oriental Heritage." *The Story of Civilization: Part I*. New York: Simon & Schuster.

Eden, Colin, Sue Jones, and David Sims. 1983. *Messing About in Problems: An Informal Structured Approach to Their Identification and Management*. Oxford, England: Pergamon Press.

Edwards, Allen L. 1984. *Experimental Design in Psychological Research*, 5th ed. New York: Addison-Wesley.

Evans, G. Edward. 1995. *Developing Library and Information Center Collections*, 3rd ed. Englewood, Colo.: Librarians Unlimited.

Feldman, Julian, and Herschel E. Kanter. 1965. "Organizational Decision Making." In James G. March, ed., *Handbook of Organizations*, pp. 614–649. Chicago: Rand McNally.

Feldman, Shai. 1981. *The Raid on Osirak: A Preliminary Assessment*. Tel Aviv: Tel Aviv University.

Fink, Steven. 1986. *Crisis Management: Planning for the Inevitable*. New York: American Management Association.

Finn, Bernard S. 1967. "Electronic Communications." In Melvin Kranzberg and Carroll W. Purcell, Jr., eds., *Technology in Western Civilization*, Vol. II, pp. 293–309. New York: Oxford University Press.

Gale, Bradley. 1992. "Gillette Escapes the Commodity Trap." In Tom Peters, ed., *Liberation Management*, pp. 661–662. New York: Alfred A. Knopf.

Garfein, Steve. 1988. "Linking Process and Product." *Manufacturing Systems*, December 24, pp. 24–25.

Gause, Donald C., and Gerald M. Weinberg. 1982. *Are Your Lights On? How to Figure Out What the Problem Really Is*. Cambridge, Mass.: Winthrop.

Georgantzas, Nicholas C., and William Acar. 1995. *Scenario-Driven Planning: Learning to Manage Strategic Uncertainty*. Westport, Conn.: Quorum.

Ghiselin, Brewster. 1955. *The Creative Process*. New York: Mentor Books.

Gilbreth, Frank. 1908. *Concrete System*. New York: Engineering New Publishing Company.

Gilbreth, Frank. 1912. *Motion Study*. New York: D. Van Nostrand.

Gordon, Michael R. 1990. "Iraq Army Invaded Capital of Kuwait in Fierce Fighting." *New York Times*, August 2, pp. A1, A8.

Granger, John V. 1979. *Technology and International Relations*. San Francisco: W.H. Freeman.

"Ground Attack Launched." 1991. *Facts on File*, Vol. 51, No. 2623, February 28, pp. 125–126.

Grove, Andrew S. 1983. *High Output Management*. New York: Random House.

Gruber, William H., and John S. Niles. 1976. *The New Management: Line and Staff Professional in the Future Firm*. New York: McGraw-Hill.

Harrison, E. Frank. 1987. *The Managerial Decision-Making Process*, 3rd ed. Boston: Houghton Mifflin.

Hartwig, Frederick, and Brian Dearing. 1979. *Explanatory Data Analysis*. Beverly Hills, Calif.: Sage.

Hathorn, Guy B., Howard R. Penniman, and Harold Zink. 1961. *Government and Politics in the United States*. Princeton, N.J.: D. Van Nostrand.

Hayes, Robert. 1983. "Qualitative Insights from Quantitative Methods." In Douglas N. Dickson, ed., *Using Logical Techniques for Making Better Decisions*, pp. 124–139. New York: John Wiley & Sons.

Heifetz, Ronald A., and Donald L. Laurie. 1997. "The Work of Leadership." *Harvard Business Review*, January–February, pp. 124–134.

Helmer, Olaf. 1967. *Analysis of the Future: The Delphi Method*. Santa Monica, Calif.: Rand Corporation.

"Hershey, Milton Snavely," article in *Encyclopedia Britannica*. 1990. Chicago: Encyclopaedia Britannica.

Hickman, Craig R., and Michael A. Silva. 1984. *Creating Excellence: Managing Corporate Culture, Strategy and Change in the New Age*. New York: A Plume Book (Penguin).

Hinrichs, Thomas R. 1992. *Problem-solving in Open Worlds: A Case Study in Design*. Hillsdale, N.J.: Lawrence Erlbaum.

Hogarth, Robin. 1987. *Judgement and Choice: The Psychology of Decision*, 2nd ed. New York: John Wiley & Sons.

Hull, C.L. 1943. *Principles of Behavior: An Introduction to Behavior Theory*. New York: Appleton-Century-Crofts.

Humble, John W. 1973. *How to Manage by Objectives*. New York: American Management Association.

"Invading Iraqis Seize Kuwait and Its Oil." 1990. *New York Times*, August 3, p. A8.

"Iraq Army Invaded Capital of Kuwait in Fierce Fighting." 1990. *New York Times*, August 2, pp. A1, A8.

"Iraq Hit by Air Strike." 1991. *Facts on File*, Vol. 51, No. 2617, January 17, p. 25.

"Iraq Forces Invade, Occupy Kuwait." 1990. *Facts on File*, Vol. 50. No. 2593, August 3, pp. 25–31.

"Israeli Warplanes Bomb Atomic Plant in Iraq." 1981. *Facts on File*, Vol. 41, No. 2117, June 12, pp. 385–386.

Jacobson, Gary, and John Hillkirk. 1987. *The Behind the Scenes Story of How a Corporation Giant Beat the Japanese at Their Own Game*. New York: Macmillan.

James, William. 1990. "Principles of Psychology." In Mortimer J. Adler, ed., *Great Books of the Western World*, Vol. 55, pp. 668–671. Chicago: University of Chicago Press.

Janis, Irving. 1989. *Crucial Decisions: Leadership in Policy Making and Crisis Management*. New York: Free Press.

Jun, Jong S., and William B. Storm, eds. 1973. *Tomorrow's Organizations: Challenge and Strategies*. Glenview, Ill.: Scott, Foresman.

Kaplan, Abraham. 1964. *The Conduct of Inquiry*. Scranton, Pa.: Chandler.

Kaufman, Roger A. 1976. *Identifying and Solving Problems: A System Approach*. San Diego: University Associates.

Kegley, Charles W., Jr., and Eugene R. Wittkopf. 1987. *American Foreign Policy: Pattern and Process*, 3rd ed. New York: St. Martin's Press.

Kennedy, Robert F. 1985. *Thirteen Days: A Memoir of the Cuban Missile Crisis*. New York: Basic Books.

Kepner, Charles H., and Benjamin B. Tregoe. 1981. *The New Rational Manager*. Princeton, N.J.: Princeton University Press.

King, Thomas. 1981. *Problem Solving in a Project Environment*. New York: John Wiley & Sons.

Kleindorfer, Paul, Howard C. Kunreuther, and Paul J.H. Schoemaker. 1993. *Decision Sciences: An Integrative Perspective*. New York: Cambridge University Press.

Knowles, Thomas W. 1989. *Management Science: Building and Using Models*. Homewood, Ill.: Irwin.

Kroeber, Donald K., and R. Lawrence LaForge. 1980. *The Manager's Guide to Statistics and Quantitative Methods*. New York: McGraw-Hill.

Kuehn, Thomas J., and Alan L. Porter, eds. 1981. *Science, Technology, and National Policy*. Ithaca, N.Y.: Cornell University Press.

Kuhn, Thomas S. 1962. *The Structure of Scientific Revolution*. Chicago: University of Chicago Press.

Laszlo, Ervin, and Christopher Laszlo. 1997. *The Insight Edge: An Introduction to the Theory and Practice of Evolutionary Management*. Westport, Conn.: Quorum.

Lave, Charles A., and James G. March. 1975. *An Introduction to Models in the Social Sciences*. New York: Harper & Row.

Lazarsfeld, Paul A. 1959. "Evidence and Inference in Social Research." In Daniel Lerner, ed., *Evidence and Inference*, pp. 107–138. Glencoe, Ill.: Free Press.

Learson, T.V. 1968. "Management of Change." *Journal of World Business*, January, pp. 59–64.

Leeds, Dorothy. 1988. *Smart Questions: A New Strategy for Successful Managers*. New York: Berkeley Books.

Leighton, Richard M. 1976. *The Great Fighter Sweepstakes: Selling the F-16 in Europe*. Washington, D.C.: Industrial College of the Armed Forces.

Lindley, D.V. 1985. *Making Decisions*, 2nd ed. New York: John Wiley & Sons.

Lindsay, Franklin. 1958. *New Techniques for Management Decision Making*. New York: McGraw-Hill.

"Lost Horizons: A Grand Tradition Can Make a Fall That Much Harder." 1991. *Wall Street Journal*, September 16, p. A1.

Lydenberg, Steven D. et al., and the Council on Economic Priorities. 1986. *Rating America's Corporate Conscience*. Reading, Mass.: Addison-Wesley.

March, James G. 1994. *A Primer on Decisionmaking: How Decisions Happen*. New York: Free Press.

Marchetti, Victor, and John D. Marks. 1974. *The CIA and the Cult of Intelligence*. New York: Alfred A. Knopf.

Margerison, Charles. 1974. *Managerial Problem Solving*. New York: McGraw-Hill.

Massie, Joseph L. 1971. *Essentials of Management*, 2nd ed. Englewood Cliffs, N.J.: Prentice-Hall.

Mattera, Philip. 1987. *Inside U.S. Business*. Homewood, Ill.: Dow, Jones, and Irwin.

McClave, James T., and Frank H.A. Ditrich. 1983. *First Course in Statistics*. San Francisco: Dellen.

McGuire, Peter, and Sara Putzell. 1989. "Defining Problems That Call for Innovation." *Technical Writing and Communication*, Vol. 19, No. 3, pp. 255–265.

McNeil, William H. 1982. *The Pursuit of Power*. Chicago: University of Chicago Press.

Merton, Robert. 1957. *Social Theory and Social Structure*. Chicago: University of Chicago Press.

Meyerson, M., and E.C. Banfield. 1955. *Politics, Planning, and the Public Interest*. Glencoe, Ill.: Free Press.

Millet, J. 1947. *The Process of Organization of Government Planning*. New York: Columbia University Press.

Mills, D. Quinn. 1996. "The Decline and Fall of IBM." *Sloan Management Review*, Vol. 37. No. 4, Summer, pp. 78–82.

Milward, Alan S. 1979. *Economy and Society: 1939–1945*. Berkeley: University of California Press.

Mintz, Alex, Nehemia Geva, Steven B. Redd, and Amy Carnes. 1997. "The Effect of Dynamic and Static Choice Sets on Political Decision Making: An Analysis Using the Decision Board Platform." *American Political Science Review*, Vol. 91, No. 3, September, pp. 553–566.

Mitchell, Stephen. 1987. *The Book of Job*. New York: Harper Perennial.

Mitroff, Ian. 1998. *Smart Thinking for Crazy Times: The Art of Solving the Right Problems*. San Francisco: Berrett-Koehler.

Moore, L.B. 1958. "How to Manage Improvement." *Harvard Business Review*, May–June, pp. 75–84.

Morgenthau, Hans J., and Kenneth W. Thompson. 1985. *Politics Among Nations: The Struggle for Power and Peace*. New York: Alfred A. Knopf.

Moskowitz, Milton, Robert Levering, and Michael Katz, eds. 1990. *Everybody's Business*. New York: Doubleday, Currency.

Myrdal, Gunnar. 1981. "The Transfer of Technology to Underdeveloped Countries." In Thomas J. Kuehn and Alan L. Porter, eds., *Science, Technology, and National Policy*, pp. 215–225. Ithaca, N.Y.: Cornell University Press.

Nadler, David A., Robert B. Shaw, and Elice A. Walton and Associates. 1995. *Discontinuous Change*. San Francisco: Jossey-Bass.

Neustadt, Richard E., and Ernest R. May. 1986. *Thinking in Time: The Uses of History for Decision Makers*. New York: Free Press.

Nutt, P.C. 1989. *Making Tough Decisions*. San Francisco: Jossey-Bass.

Oden, Howard W. 1997. *Managing Corporate Culture, Innovation, and Entrepreneurship*. Westport, Conn.: Quorum.

Osborn, Alex. 1949. *Your Creative Power*. New York: Charles Scribner's Sons.

Oster, Patrick. 1991. "European Auto Industry in Race Against Imports." *Washington Post*, December 29, pp. H1, H5.

O'Toole, James. 1995. *Leading Change: Overcoming the Ideology of Comfort and the Tyranny of Custom*. San Francisco: Jossey-Bass.

Ouchi, William. 1981. *Theory Z: How American Business Can Meet the Japanese Challenge*. Reading, Mass.: Addison-Wesley.

Palmer, R.R., and Joel Colton. 1984. *A History of the Modern World*, 6th ed. New York: McGraw-Hill.

"Pan Am Seeks Chapter 11 Shield, Gets UAL-Backed Cash Infusion." 1991. *Wall Street Journal*, January 9, p. A3.

"Pan Am to Cut Its Work Force by 15% and Further Reduce Service to Europe." 1991. *Wall Street Journal*, February 6, p. A5.

"Pan Am Unit's Traffic Declines." 1991. *Wall Street Journal*, May 6, p. C5.

"Pan Am's December Traffic Fell." 1991. *Wall Street Journal*, January 7, p. A4.

Parnes, Sidney J., and Harold F. Harding, eds. 1962. *A Source Book for Creative Thinking*. New York: Charles Scribner's Sons.

Patchett, Isabel S. 1982. *Statistical Methods for Managers and Administrators*. New York: Van Nostrand Reinhold.

Pauly, D. 1976. "Aviation: A Troubled Bird." *Newsweek*, June 7, p. 73.

Peters, Thomas J., and Robert H. Waterman. 1982. *In Search of Excellence: Lessons from America's Best-Run Companies*. New York: Warner Books.

Peters, Tom. 1992. *Liberation Management*. New York: Alfred A. Knopf.

"Piaget, Jean," article in *Encyclopaedia Britannica*. 1990. Chicago: Encyclopedia Britannica.

Picken, Joseph C., and Gregory G. Dess. 1998. "Right Strategy—Wrong Problem." *Organizational Dynamics*, Summer, pp. 35–49.

Plous, S. 1993. *The Psychology of Judgment and Decision Making*. New York: McGraw-Hill.

Plunkett, Lorne, and Guy A. Hale. 1982. *The Proactive Manager: The Complete Book of Problem-solving and Decision Making*. New York: Wiley-Interscience.

Prahalad, C.K., and Richard Bettis. 1986. "The Dominant Logic: A New Linkage Between Diversity and Performance." *Strategic Management Journal*, Vol. 7, pp. 485–501.

Praskash, S., and Mike H. Ryan. 1979. *Dresser Industries Inc*. Boston: Harvard Business School.

"Progress." 1990. In Mortimer J. Adler, ed., *Great Books of the Western World*, Vol. 2, pp. 349–356. Chicago: University of Chicago Press.

Pruitt, Steve, and Tom Barrett. 1991. "Corporate Virtual Workspace." In Michael Benediki, ed., *Cyberspace: First Steps*, pp. 37–52. Cambridge, Mass.: MIT Press.

Rae, John B. 1967. "The Rationalization of Production." In Melvin Kranzberg and Carroll W. Purcell, Jr., *Technology in Western Civilization*, Vol. II, pp. 37–52. New York: Oxford University Press.

Rao, S.R. 1973. "An Example of the Third World." *New Scientist*, August 23, pp. 451–452.

Redden, W.J. 1971. *Effective Management by Objectives*. New York: McGraw-Hill.

Rerick, Mark N. 1978. *Problem Solving: A Systems Approach*. Princeton, N.J.: Petrocelli Books.

Revelle, Roger. 1981. "The Scientist and the Politician." In Thomas J. Kuehn and Alan L. Porter, eds., *Science, Technology, and National Policy*, pp. 142–143. Ithaca, N.Y.: Cornell University Press.

Reynolds, E.C. 1968. *The Field Is Won: The Life and Death of Saint Thomas More*. Milwaukee, Wis.: Bruce.

Ries, A., and Jack Trout. 1986. *Marketing Warfare*. New York: McGraw-Hill.

Robertshaw, Joseph E., Stephen Mecca, and Mark N. Rerick. 1978. *Problem Solving: A Systems Approach*. Princeton, N.J.: Petrocelli Books.

Rogers, David, Jr. 1987. *Waging Business Warfare*. New York: Charles Scribner's Sons.

Rowe, Alan J., and Richard Mason. 1987. *Managing with Style*. San Francisco: Jossey-Bass.

Rubin, Irene S., and Lana Stein. 1990. "Budget Reform in St. Louis: Why Does Budgeting Change?" *Public Administration Review*, July–August, pp. 424–427.

Rumler, G.A., and A.P. Brache. 1990. *Improving Performance*. San Francisco: Jossey-Bass.

Russo, J. Edward, and Paul J.H. Schoemaker. 1989. *Decision Traps: The Ten Barriers to Brilliant Decision-Making and How to Overcome Them*. New York: Simon & Schuster.

Rutman, Leonard, ed. 1977. *Evaluation Research Methods*. Beverly Hills, Calif.: Sage.

Sabine, George. 1950. *A History of Political Philosophy*. New York: Henry Holt.

Sardar, Ziauddin, and Dauwud G. Rosser-Owen. 1977. "Science Policy and Developing Countries." In Ina Spiegel-Rösing and Derek de Solla Price, eds., *Science, Technology and Society*, pp. 535–575. Beverly Hills, Calif.: Sage.

Sampson, Anthony. 1984. *Empires of the Sky: The Politics, Contests and Cartels of World Airlines*. New York: Random House.

Sanders, Ralph. 1957. "Nuclear Electrification for Latin America." Ph.D. diss., Georgetown University.

Sanders, Ralph. 1973. *The Politics of Defense Analysis*. New York: Dunellen.

Sanders, Ralph, ed. 1975. *Science and Technology: Vital National Resources*. Mt. Airy, Md.: Lomond Books.

Sanders, Ralph. 1979. "Bureaucratic Ploys and Stratagems: The Case of the U.S. Department of Defense." *Jerusalem Journal of International Relations*, Vol. 4, No. 2, pp. 1–14.

Sanders, Ralph. 1983. *International Dynamics of Technology*. Westport, Conn.: Greenwood Press.

Sanders, Ralph. 1987. "Penetrating the Fog of Technology's Social Dimensions." *Technology in Society*, Vol. 9, pp. 163–180.

Sax, I. 1971. *Defending the Environment*. New York: Alfred A. Knopf.

Scheffler, Israel. 1963. *The Anatomy of Inquiry*. Indianapolis, Ind.: Bobbs-Merrill.

Schick, Allen. 1990. "Budgeting for Results: Recent Developments in Five Industrialized Countries." *Public Administration Review*, January–February, pp. 26–33.

Schoennauer, Alfred W. 1981. *Problem Finding and Problem-solving*. Chicago: Nelson-Hall.

Schwartz, John. 1998. "Thalidomide Wins Limited Approval." *Washington Post*, July 17, pp. A1, A14.

Schwartz, Joshua Ira. 1979. "Smallpox Immunization: Controversial Episodes." In Dorothy Nelkin, ed., *Controversy: Politics of Technical Decisions*, pp. 181–193. Beverly Hills, Calif.: Sage.

Seaborg, Glenn T., and William R. Corliss. 1971. *Man and Atom*. New York: Dutton.

"Senator Claiborne of Rhode Island." 1990. *New York Times*, August 3, p. A8.

Sherwin, Douglas. 1988. "Management by Objectives." *Harvard Business Review*, May–June, pp. 149–160.

Shorter Oxford University Dictionary. 1989. Oxford, England: Clarendon Press.

Simon, George T. 1981. *The Big Bands*, 4th ed. New York: Schirmer Books.

Simon, Herbert. 1957. *Administrative Behavior*, 2nd ed. New York: Macmillan.

Simon, Herbert. 1960. *New Science of Management Decision*. New York: Harper & Bros.

Sims, R.R. 1994. *Ethics and Organizational Decision Making: A Call for Renewal*. Westport, Conn.: Quorum.

Smirchich, Linda, and Charles Stubbart. 1985. "Strategic Management in an Enacted World." *Academy of Management Review*, Vol. 10, No. 4, pp. 724–736.

Smith, Thomas M. 1969. "Origins of the Computer." In Melvin Kranzberg and Carroll W. Purcell, Jr., eds., *Technology in Civilization*, Vol. 2, pp. 309–323. New York: Oxford University Press.

Sobel, C. Robert. 1981. *IBM: Colossus in Transition*. New York: Truman Tallery Books.

Spiegel-Rosing, Ina, and Derek de Solla Price, eds. 1977. *Science, Technology and Society: A Cross-Disciplinary Perspective*. Beverly Hills, Calif.: Sage.

Spirer, Herbert F. 1975. *Business Statistics: A Problem-solving Approach*. Homewood, Ill.: Irwin.

Steele, Lowell W. 1975. *Innovation in Big Business*. New York: Elsevier.

Steiner, G., ed. 1965. *The Creative Organization*. Chicago: University of Chicago Press.

Stevenson, William. 1989. *Introduction to Management Science*. Homewood, Ill.: Irwin.

Szyliowicz, Joseph, ed. 1981. *Technology and International Affairs*. New York: Praeger.

Taylor, Frederick. 1912. *The Principles of Scientific Management*. New York: Harper's.

Thierauf, Robert. 1987. *A Problem-Finding Approach to Effective Corporate Planning*. Westport, Conn.: Quorum.

Timms, Howard L. 1967. *Introduction to Management Science*. Homewood, Ill.: Irwin.

Toffler, Alvin. 1980. *The Third Wave*. New York: William Morrow.

Tuma, D.T., and R. Reif. 1980. *Problem-solving and Education: Issues in Teaching and Research*. Hillsdale, N.J.: Lawrence Erlbaum.

Turban, Efraim. 1988. *Decision Support and Expert Systems: Managerial Perspectives*. New York: Macmillan.

Twiss, Brian. 1974. *Managing Technological Innovation*. New York: Longman.

"U.N. Condemns Israel for Raid on Iraq A Plant." 1981. *Facts on File*, Vol. 41, No. 2119, June 26, pp. 434–435.

Urbaniak, Douglas. 1991. "Integrated Program Management Support System Is Key to Automotive Future." *Project Management Journal*, September, pp. 17–21.

U.S. House. 1969. Committee on Science and Astronautics, Subcommittee on Science, Research and Development. *Congressional Concern with the Decline and Fall of Mohole Technological Information for U.S. Congress*. Report prepared by the Science Policy Research Division Legislative Reference Service. 91st Cong., 1st sess., April 25.

U.S. Senate. 1961. Committee on Government Operations, Subcommittee on National Policy Machinery. *Organizing for National Security, State Defense and National Security Council*. 87th Cong., 1st sess.

"U.S.-Led Coalition Attacks Iraq After UN Deadline for Withdrawal from Kuwait Passes." 1991. *Facts on File*, Vol. 51, No. 2617, January 17, pp. 25–31.

Van Gundy, Arthur. 1981. *Techniques of Structured Problem-solving*. New York: D. Van Nostrand.

Walden, Gene, and Edmund O. Lawler. 1993. *Marketing Masters: Secrets of America's Best Companies*. New York: Harper Business References.

Wallsten, T.S., ed. 1980. *Cognitive Processes in Choice and Decision Behavior*. Hillsdale, N.J.: Lawrence Erlbaum.

Walsh, Myles E. 1981. *Understanding Computers: What Managers and Users Need to Know*. New York: Wiley-Interscience.

Watson, Thomas J. 1963. *A Business and Its Beliefs: The Ideas That Helped Build IBM*. New York: McGraw-Hill.

Watson, Thomas J. 1990. *Father, Son & Co.* New York: Bantam Books.

Whtye, G. 1991. "Decision Failures: Why They Occur and How to Prevent Them." *Academy of Management Executives*, Vol. 5, No. 3, pp. 23–29.

Wise, A.S. 1966. "IBM's $5 Billion Gamble," *Fortune*, October 7, pp. 118–123.

Wohlstetter, Roberta. 1962. *Pearl Harbor: Warning and Decision*. Palo Alto, Calif.: Stanford University Press.

Yukl, Gary. 1994. *Leadership in Organizations*, 3rd ed. Englewood Cliffs, N.J.: Prentice-Hall.

Zahra, Shaker, and Sherry Chaples. 1993. "Blind Spots in Competitive Analysis." *Academy of Management Executive*, Vol. 7, No. 2, pp. 7–28.

Zajac, Edward, and Max Bazerman. 1991. "Blind Spots in Industry and Competitor Analysis: Implications of Interfirm (Mis)perceptions for Strategic Decisions." *Academy of Management Review*, Vol. 16, No. 1, pp. 37–56.

Index

About the Author

RALPH SANDERS is J. Carlton Ward, Jr. Distinguished Professor Emeritus at the National Defense University/Industrial College of the Armed Forces. He taught part-time at American University and at Johns Hopkins University, and served at the White House and on the staff of the secretary of defense. He is the recipient of the Army's highest civilian award. He has published extensively, including the books *Arms Industries: New Supplies and Regional Security* (1990) and *International Dynamics of Technology* (Greenwood Press, 1983).

ISBN 1-56720-293-4

90000>

EAN

9 781567 202939

HARDCOVER BAR CODE